MY LIVERPOOL SCHOOLS

Norman Bridge

Published in 1992 by The Kirkland Press, Causey Mount, Dorothy Well, Portinscale CA12 5RQ.

ISBN 0 9518544 0 2

Printed by Birkenhead Press Limited, 1-3 Grove Road, Rock Ferry, Birkenhead, Merseyside L42 3XS.

CONTENTS

ILLUSTRATIONS

to my colleagues

'The great skill of a teacher is to get and keep the attention of his scholar; whilst he has that, he is sure to advance as fast as the learner's abilities will carry him, and without that, all his hustle and pother will be to little or no purpose. To attain this he should make the child comprehend (as much as may be) the usefulness of what he teaches him, and let him see by what he has learnt that he can do something which he could not do before, something which gives him some power and real advantage over others who are ignorant of it. To this he should add sweetness in all his instructions, and by a certain tenderness in his whole carriage make the child sensible that he loves him and designs nothing but his good, the only way to beget love in the child which will make him hearken to his lessons and relish what he teaches him.'

John Locke (1632-1704)

'A school is like the world. Only government can prevent brutal violence.'

Bertrand Russell (1872-1970)

FOREWORD

They were all in Liverpool. From Victorian red-brick, when Liverpool people boasted it was the second port of the Empire, and the Cunard and White Star ocean-going liners towered over the Landing Stage, to the award winning architects' designs of a Liverpool known for its two cathedrals and the Beatles. From the era of chalk and gaslight to a sophisticated array of teaching aids — the projector, record player, radio, tape recorder, television, language laboratory, and the first flickering of the computer. From the obedient pupils of the 1920's to the less respectful of the 1970's. Was it progress? Perhaps these reminiscences of an insider will help the onlooker to judge.

THE COUNCIL SCHOOLS (1)

My mother took me to the first one, Birchfield Road school in the Fairfield district, an immense — to me — red brick building. It was, I discovered later, one of a group of 'Principal' schools, built to house three departments — infants, juniors, and seniors. Each department had a Head Teacher. The Principal was in charge of the whole school. A child would spend its entire school life in this one building. We went along one afternoon towards the end of the summer term to have a look at it from the outside. This happened to be at the end of the school day. Out of one of the doors emerged a group of shouting running boys, like a mob on the rampage. I wondered what I was in for.

On the first day of the autumn term 1916 she took me. Her hand was about level with my ear, and my right hand was stretched up holding hers. Having no sisters, I noticed on the other side of the road a girl of my own age, with golden hair which waved up and down as she ran. Her name. was Edie Partington. I wonder what happened to her. The first class was known as the babies' class. We would learn the beginnings of number and reading, but I remember best the sand table with its coloured models of animals and houses, and the knitting lesson. In over, through, off — the skill has lasted a

Birchfield Road School

lifetime. I liked the Headmistress, Miss Dawson. She moved about in a smiling friendly way. I felt safe with her.

The assembly hall seemed vast. Large, lofty, with overhead roof lighting and a balcony around giving access to classrooms, and at one end staircases, not used by the pupils, but by the Principal to take assembly. The Principal, Mr Smith, seemed to me a stern, imposing figure. I was to meet him later as a student, when he told me that the art of teaching was in overcoming the scholar's reluctance to learn. But for a small boy it was a solemn moment to see him moving in his black gown slowly up the stairs, a bald head over sunken eyes and beetling brows, turning, as he reached the platform half way up, to the assembled school, when there was an immediate silence and the service began. There was morning assembly, and evening assembly at the end of the day. I remember the evening assembly better than the morning assembly, and the hymns still echo sadly down the years — 'Now the day is over' — 'The day thou gavest, Lord, is ended'.

Class teaching, after the babies' class was straightforward and methodical. We were made to put our hands on our heads or behind our backs, so that we would give full attention to the teacher. Arithmetic tables and spelling were taught by rote. My only brush with authority at that tender age was when, during morning playtime, a group of senior girls decided to do a little teaching practice of their own and got together a few of us youngsters in the cloakroom, divided us into groups and taught us poems. I recall 'When you come to the end of a perfect day, And sit alone with your thoughts'. When the staff got wind of this, the girls were packed off into the playground and we were told we must not take part in such activities again.

The school, like most schools then, was orderly and progressive. Memories are unaccountable and sporadic. I recall a lesson in which a teacher, when the subject would be history, told us that a war was going on and at that moment soldiers of the two sides were facing each other in the trenches. Due to war-time reorganisation, Mr Smith was transferred to a Grammar School in the city centre and his successor was Mr Hallam, a tall, kindly man. One soon learnt that amongst us the teachers were referred to as 'Ma' for the ladies and 'Daddy' for the men. So it was that Daddy Crawford had been seen standing outside the public house wiping his lips with a handkerchief. In those days, this was a matter for parental concern. Ma Hill was crabby, she stood no nonsense. I passed at Birchfield two uneventful and contented years.

At that time, during the shortage of men teachers away on war service, my mother decided to return to teaching and took an appointment at Clint Road School in the Edge Hill district. She also decided that I should move from Birchfield Road to Clint Road. Clint Road was a very different school. An older building without an assembly hall and the facilities which later were put into new schools.

The Headmaster, Mr Clarke, was businesslike and efficient. He was a good example of the two-year trained teacher from the teacher training colleges. The literature of education does not appear to pay tribute to the excellent products of that system. They staffed the so-called Council Schools throughout the country until, later on in the century, more graduates came into the secondary schools and, of course, the face of secondary education changed. They were men and women who, later on, would on their merits have gone through University. They knew their subjects to the required standard and, above all, they were capable and, with experience, skilful teachers in the classroom. As has often been remarked in staffrooms, a University degree is not a guarantee of teaching ability.

Mr Clarke did the rounds of his classrooms regularly, wearing his bowler hat which came on and off during his progress. Our age group at that time was too young to judge and comment upon staff idiosyncrasies, a traditional and therapeutic occupation of school pupils throughout the ages. At Clint Road, at that time, as in all schools, the cane was a normal and accepted part of school life. Boys who gave enough trouble were sent down to Mr Clarke for the appropriate response. It was established practice that when one had had the cane, one returned to the classroom blowing the hands and beating the arms against the sides to show the severity of the punishment and the fortitude of the sufferer. Some enterprising lads would return to class performing this pantomime without having visited the Head. Inevitably this happened one afternoon when the Head was already in the classroom. Our sympathies went out to the unfortunate fellow as he was led away. In the winter as it grew dark in the late afternoon a welcome diversion was provided by the caretaker. The overhead gaslighting was controlled by a crossbar, from the ends of which hung chains with a ring attached. Carrying a five foot pole topped by a flame from an oil-fed wick and a hook, he pulled down the correct end of the crossbar with the hook, and applied the flame to the gas mantle. As we all watched closely, hey presto, the mantle exploded into light.

In the playground there were seasons: buttons, spinning tops, cherry stones (known as cherry wobs). The seasons waxed and waned, following each other by an immutable and unaccountable law of change. In the button season, buttons — mostly metal trouser buttons — were won or lost by a routine of pitch and toss. In the tops season, the brightly coloured tops of different designs were sent spinning and whirling by our whips. No-one interfered with anyone else's top, which might land unexpectedly nearby. The most interesting season was cherry wobs. We sat with our backs against the wall and our legs spreadeagled to accommodate our apparatus. Some had prepared a piece of wood with openings of different sizes, like gateways. The smallest one might have the figure 5 over it,the larger ones 0. You threw your cherry wob and got your return according to the hole it went through. The intellectuals had a device like a roulette board, divided into segments. Many of the segments were marked 0, one or two 5, and the other figures in between. A needle like a compass needle was mounted, which was blown and revolved to rest upon your number, when, having paid your entry fee, you received your winnings, or not. Most had a bottle cork which was placed on the ground between the legs to be knocked over by throwing a cherry wob, while the owner shouted 'One and your own back', 'two and your own back', 'three and your own back', according to the competition. The entrepreneurs would stick a piece of chewing gum under the cork.

Towards the end of the morning of the 11th November 1918, we were told that at 11 o'clock that morning, an Armistice had been signed between the Allies and the Germans and that the war was over. Although, as I recall, there was no mention of victory or defeat, it was a matter for general rejoicing and we were sent home for the day. It was a sunny, still, cold day, and as I turned the corner from Edge Lane into Beech Street, I stopped and reflected that this was a historic day which I should remember. The following summer, a Peace Treaty had been signed and we were taken to the pictures, as the cinema was then called, followed by a beanfeast of tea, cakes and scones. Later in the year, an eclipse of the sun brought a pleasing diversion from the school routine. We were told not to look with the naked eye. The weather was kind, the sky cloudless, and as we went back into school, after viewing the eclipse through our smoked pieces of glass and photographic negatives, we hoped that this agreeable event would happen more often.

At that time — it was only thirty-nine years after elementary education became legally compulsory — there was concern that able children should have the education of which they were capable, unhindered by lack of resources. The city's schools consisted largely of Council Schools, taking children from the age of five to fourteen. These co-existed with a small number of Secondary Schools, later called Grammar Schools, which took pupils to external examination standard and University entrance. The Education Committee had established a system of Junior City Scholarships and free places to ease the passage from Council to Secondary School. Senior City Scholarships were from Secondary School to University. The thinking at that time was that if a child was clever enough, he or she should go up, either within a school, or from Council School to Secondary School. Clever children would find themselves in class with their elders, while the slow learners would be with their juniors.

At the age of nine I was told that I was to sit for the scholarship. There was a special coaching group in school, and my mother saw that I did the homework in the evening. I remember the mental fatigue of those days, particularly after evening homework. The examination took place at the

Oulton Secondary School near the city centre. I recall arithmetic problems that would no doubt baffle me today, and an essay. During the mid-morning break, presumably in the absence of a playground, we were allowed to go out into the street. I explored a little, and looked down the hill at a massive grey building. This, I later discovered, was the Adelphi Hotel. I was also entered for a special reading prize. The audition took place at the Liverpool Education Office. I remember a dark room and two or three smiling men, smiling, no doubt at my diminutive stature. This was my first entry into the building in Sir Thomas Street, where, in later years, I was to be a frequent visitor. Some weeks later Mr. Clarke sent for me. I had, as it was said at the time, won a scholarship and the reading prize to boot. I was to go immediately and tell my mother, who was then teaching at my original school, Birchfield Road. There I was allowed to go up to mother's classroom, where she was taking a class, seated in the high single combined desk and seat which were the fashion then. I gave her the news. She was so carried away that she informed the class. They received the information with admirable calm.

The prizegiving was held in the Central Hall in Renshaw Street. The chief guest was the Reverend Dr. W. R. Inge, Dean of St Paul's, an outstanding scholar and previously Professor of Divinity at Cambridge. He was later known, because of his pessimistic sermons and newspaper articles, as the Gloomy Dean. It was said that he had received a letter from a lady who wrote, 'I hate your sermons and loathe your views. I am praying for your death. I have been successful in three other cases.' Nevertheless the Dean lived another thirty-three years, to die at the age of ninety-four. As he bent over to present my prize, I was conscious of a pale, lean figure, surmounting a pair of knee breeches and gaiters, all in black.

THE GRAMMAR SCHOOL

The Liverpool Institute — the Secondary School which my parents had chosen for me — was by Liverpool standards an old foundation, having been opened in 1825 as the Liverpool Mechanics Institute. The Mechanics Institutes were the outcome of the initiative of George Birbeck, a Quaker and Lecturer at Anderson's Institute in Glasgow. His experience there convinced him of the demand and need for further education for working men. He formed a 'mechanics class' which developed into a Mechanics Institute in 1823. Similar establishments were opened in London and elsewhere, and their success confirmed Birbeck's assessment.

The Institute building was then nearly 100 years old. It had — and still has — an imposing main entrance, fronted by a large pillared classical portico. The door led to an entrance space leading to two large wrought iron gates. Beyond lay the assembly hall, where the benches, tiered in a U-shape, radiated from the platform like a Greek theatre. The balcony followed the same pattern. There was room for 600-700 without overcrowding. The organ, poised miraculously above the platform, was played from a console at the side — a technical achievement which mystified us. It was

The Liverpool Institute.

played by the Mathematics Master, a gentleman of lugubrious countenance and sombre dress. I felt sorry for him, thinking he had suffered great misfortune. The back windows looked out on to the young and growing Liverpool Cathedral, the foundation stone of which had been laid only seventeen years previously by King Edward VII.

I was taken on the first day by my brother, who was then in the Lower Sixth. I suspect he didn't quite know what to do with me when we got there, and was relieved when I bolted from his side to join some of my pals from the previous school. With them, I was put in form 3X — 'X' standing for 'Express'. The idea was that we bright boys would cover in four years a five year course leading to the School Certificate and Matriculation, the equivalent of today's GCSE. I found that I was the youngest in the form, a position which was to last until I was in the Upper Sixth. Happily in later years, it was realised that for schoolchildren organised in classes, maturity takes priority over academic ability and transfers by ability were only within similar age groups.

The Headmaster was H. V. Whitehouse, a bearded, imposing figure. Of German extraction, he had begun life with the name Weisse, which he had understandably changed to Whitehouse during the war. In a laboratory accident he had lost three fingers of one hand. The forefinger seemed to have grown longer in compensation and we were intrigued to see him use it to grasp objects with a kind of corkscrew movement. My only contact with him was brief and explosive. Under the impression that absence notes had to be taken direct to the Head, I went at the beginning of morning school to his study. An indicator board beside the door, switched on from inside, displayed either 'enter' or 'engaged.' It was blank and I knocked on the door. There was no response and I knocked on the door again. The 'enter' sign lit up. I opened the door. He roared at me. I fled.

For teachers in Secondary Schools, it was a time of secure and long tenure. Teaching in such a school must have been congenial, and perhaps prestigious, and it was not uncommon for staff to stay two decades or more. My brother had not been slow to entertain the family with his version of their eccentricities as and when they occurred. I felt I already knew some of them. By modern standards, discipline would have been easy. There was more respect in society for schooling and school teachers. Deterrents were graded; order marks for minor offences, if collected too quickly, led to detention on Wednesday afternoon. A 'Wednesday' could be awarded directly. Before the unrepentant wrongdoer lay the prospect of a caning from the Headmaster, or even expulsion. On one occasion in the early twenties, the school was assembled to witness a public expulsion. A boy had been found rifling through overcoat pockets in the staff cloakroom. He was made to stand on the platform while the Head gave an account of what had happened. It was probably about that time that the practice was discontinued.

It seems that teachers are remembered for their personality rather than their efficiency, though the one need not exclude the other. There was Paul Duffy, the Irishman. We liked the way he handled the Crippled Girls Fund. It was by means of this elusive charity that we were taught to think of others less fortunate than ourselves. Paul would get the list of contributors out and go through it by name, with expletives as appropriate. 'Good God, Jones, you haven't given a cent this term.' The holy ones smiled with smug satisfaction. Time had obscured the origin of the nickname of 'Piggy' Elliot, the Geography Master. 'Put your dirty little fingers on China' he would cry. We complied happily. We knew he was on our side. At the back of the room was a large slide projector, mounted on a tripod. The light was produced by an electric current passed between two carbon rods. As Piggy tried to adjust these to the optimum distance apart, there was a pleasing succession of hisses and flashes. While this was going on he would announce, 'This is the sort of show, gentlemen, where you need a good orchestra.' I remember with gratitude H. M. Brown, who taught middle school English. He loved English Literature and he loved teaching it. He would leave his desk, come to the front of the class, put a foot on a vacant chair and hold his book with elbow on knee and illuminate for us the current book, Macbeth, Travels with a Donkey. His face and the cut of his moustache recalled Robert Louis Stevenson, who perhaps for him was a hero and a father figure. I last saw him some years later,

H.M. Brown's Fifth Form at the Liverpool Institute. The author is on the front row, extreme right.

when he must have been well into middle age, walking along the Wirral seashore with his wife, their arms linked together. Generally the staff were a tolerant lot, well equipped academically to teach their subject to the required standard. Probably none of them had taken a course of teacher training. It is doubtfūl whether, after their first few months of service, their performance would have been much different if they had.

In due course, it became known that H. V. Whitehouse was to retire and there was much speculation as to the identity of his successor. One morning I was sent to the school office on a message. I overheard one of the office staff say to a colleague, 'He is a parson and his name is Symonds.' Returning to the classroom, I enjoyed briefly the prestige of a bearer of inside information.

The Reverend H. H. Symonds was educated at Rugby School and at Oriel College, Oxford, where he graduated with first class honours in Classics. He held teaching posts at Clifton and his old school Rugby before passing to a Headship at King's School, Chester, and in 1924, to the Liverpool Institute. His horizons were wider than his undisputed mastery of the Classics. He took the Sixth on Saturday mornings for what were later called 'liberal studies.' I recall one of our text books 'The Clash of Colour' at a time when there was talk of the 'Yellow Peril', a danger supposed to threaten from the teeming populations of the Far East. There were slide lectures on sculpture and painting.

Greek and Roman architecture was supplemented by a tour of Liverpool's noteworthy buildings. He taught us to look at the tops of the buildings, generally more interesting and informative than the bottom. And there was — perhaps one of the earliest — a talk on sex.

Outside Education, he was best known for his devotion to the countryside and in particular the Lake District. He pioneered the establishment of a chain of Youth Hostels in North Wales and passed on his enthusiasm to a succession of schoolboys at the summer camps he established in Borrowdale and the Duddon Valley. It may be noted in passing that at the age of fifty he gave up his headship, and retired to the Lake District, and devoted the rest of his life to the causes he loved, the preservation of natural beauty and the promotion of national parks.

Though as scholars we were not aware of it, with hindsight it seems that the new broom swept clean. The annual sports was moved from summer to the end of the spring term, no doubt to avoid clashing with examinations. Prefects turned out with canes held horizontally to keep the spectators in line. By an unkind fate it was a cold March day. The following issue of the School Magazine carried an anonymous suggestion that the next sports should be held on Christmas Day, and that the Officers Training Corps should be in attendance with fixed bayonets. But such growing pains were quickly absorbed into a liberal and enlightened regime, over which he presided during the eleven years of his Headship.

At the end of the first year half of us were moved out of the express stream into the ordinary streams. After three years we began the first moves towards specialisation, Classics — Latin and Greek, Modern — French and German, or Science — Physics and Chemistry. In contrast to today's practice we were not asked to make a choice or express a preference. I found myself in the Classical Remove. At the end of the fourth year the first external examination was taken — the School Certificate. The grades were Fail, Pass, Credit and Distinction. Five Credits carried the additional award of Matriculation.

Next year into the Lower Classical Sixth, where our Form Master was A. G. Russell, fresh from university and a short teaching spell in the south. He was later to become Head Master of the Holt Grammar School, named after one of the families who became wealthy and influential on the rising tide of Liverpool's prosperity at the end of the 19th and the beginning of the 20th century. A fine library at the Institute was the gift of Lawrence D. Holt. A Latin inscription in the library began with his initials — 'Libros dum habebimus...' (while we have books). There followed three years in the Upper Classical Sixth under the tutelage of W. R. G. Eustace, precise and occasionally sharp tongued. He was not to be trifled with.

It was about this time that one began to appreciate the many extra-curricular activities organised by some of the staff for us in their spare time. There were the usual games and athletics. There was a strong drama tradition. Each year, some forms would present a one act play, to be performed in front of the school. There were favourites which appeared more than once — "The Bishop's Candlesticks", "The Boy Comes Home", "The Grand Cham's Diamond", and John Drinkwater's "X=0". The Literary and Debating Society, which met in the evening, gave the clever and articulate a chance to shine and the timid the opportunity to aspire. The annual Hobby Show revealed a wide range of hidden talents from advanced piano playing to illuminated manuscript writing. The Officers Training Corps was intended to provide a reserve for later Army service. We dressed in the uniform of the infantryman of World War I. Our shining boots had to be laced crosswise, not herringbone fashion. We learned to wind the puttees evenly from ankle to knee. Weekly, after afternoon break, we reported in the playground for squad drill, sometimes taken by a professional sergeant from Seaforth Barracks whose incomprehensible orders we decided were in a foreign language. The Annual Field Day on the sports field in Greenbank Park qualified for a visit from the War Office, as the Ministry of Defence was then called. After taking the salute, the officer chosen for this duty watched our drill and manoeuvres. I recall we attacked, in diamond formation, an invisible enemy. The proceedings closed with an address to the troops. While we could not understand every word, we gathered that the general drift was the importance of esprit de corps. After a route march, with full kit, rifle and bayonet, from West Kirby in the Wirral to Thurstaston Hill, it was convenient to let us take our rifles home, where we did our best to impress our families with our martial expertise.

Well-known people, who would have something to say for our benefit, were invited to talk to us. I recall the Reverend 'Tubby' Clayton, co-founder of Toc H, an organisation for Christian Fellowship, founded at Poperinghe in Belgium in 1915 during the early dark days of the First World War. The explorer, Sir Francis Younghusband, then in his sixties, had led an expedition to Tibet which introduced it to the Western World. He brought a group of Tibetan monks with their bells and long horns, too long and heavy to hold, the front end resting on the floor. They made a mournful sound, but to us — not yet sophisticated by radio and television — it was a startling and memorable experience.

The Liverpool Playhouse, at that time, enjoyed a golden age. Under its director, William Armstrong, a number of actors and actresses, later to become famous, passed across its stage, Michael Redgrave, Derek Guyler, Rex Harrison among them. Mr. Eustace, whom we have already met as Master of the Classical Sixth, was an enthusiastic member of the playreading circle attached to the Theatre. We were impressed when he brought to the school a one-act play, the cast including William Armstrong and himself.

During three years in the Upper Sixth, I was to make an acquaintance with the languages and history of Ancient Greece and Rome. Latin was an exact and unforgiving language, reflecting the discipline of the Roman armies and the scope of its legal system. The Greeks, divided by the mountains into independent city-states, were quarrelsome but not warlike, except for untypical Sparta, where boys were reared for toughness and courage (it is recorded that weakling infants were taken to the hillside and left to die). Alexander the Great, who led his victorious army through Persia to India, came from Macedon in the north, beyond the circle of city-states. The Greek language, softer and more flexible than Latin, seemed fashioned to convey the culture of fifth and fourth century Greece, centred in Athens. There, in the Mediterranean sunshine, waited on by their womenfolk and their slaves, Plato, Socrates and their friends discussed at length the problems of philosophy and society, while the dramatists presented in the amphitheatres the tragedies and comedies of human nature.

The adolescent mind could only dimly appreciate the historical significance of all this, and our mental energies were fully occupied in coping with the grammar syntax and vocabularies of the languages. The weekly exercises in composition and translation scored a gamma, a beta or an alpha. The occasional alpha in the third year made us feel that we were approaching competence.

I knew that the end of the third year in the sixth form would mean the end of schoolboy life. Of a year's leavers, one or two might pass to Oxbridge after a highly competitive examination. A few would go to Redbrick universities with scholarships or grants based on the result of the Higher School Certificate. Some to industry and commerce, perhaps to one of the great shipping lines which then occupied an important place in the Liverpool business community, and some of which had established by endowments a link with the school. Those successful in gaining university awards were not notified by post, but by an announcement in the newspaper, the Liverpool Daily Post.

I left at the end of the summer term not knowing what the immediate future would be. Surprisingly, I cannot remember a leaving ceremony. It seems that we just went home on the last day. Nevertheless, I now appreciate, as many do in later life, the formative influence of those eight years, and recall the challenge of the school motto — 'Non nobis solum, sed toti mundo nati' — 'Born not for ourselves alone, but for the whole world'.

At this time I left another school. My mother was a third generation Primitive Methodist, my father a church organist. Chapel was part of life, and I had attended Sunday School from an early age. It was held in the basement of a small chapel in Jubilee Drive in the Kensington district. Year by year the age groups moved up a class. The bible class for teenagers was in a separate room. Despite the name, the Primitive Methodists were moderate and reasonable in the expression of their faith. They had parted from the Wesleyans to set up a more democratic church organisation. The Wesleyans, they thought, smacked too much of the Anglican hierarchy.

The Sunday School teachers were caring people. Most of them performed their self-imposed duty over several years. I had left bible class and had been Secretary for a year or two when I realised that my doubts were becoming stronger than my beliefs. The years of acceptance had run their course, and adult judgement had arrived. At Sunday School I was now out of place. Religion had never been thrust upon me, and my parents accepted the situation without demur.

In the late 1970's we were driving past the chapel, which we saw now belonged to the Elim Pentecostal Church, and noticed that the door of the basement was open. I went in, crossed the floor, and mounted the familiar wooden stairs. In the bible classroom a man was laying floor tiles. I passed through the minister's vestry and out into the church, as I had seen ministers and lay preachers do many times on their way to the pulpit. It was as it used to be, except that the organ had gone. Sitting in the pew which had been ours, in my imagination the families of the past took their places in their pews. The man who had been tile laying came to investigate. On hearing my credentials he returned, saying 'I'll leave you with your thoughts'.

On the way out he was waiting. I described the past, and he told me of their plans to restore the building. We were standing in the middle of the floor space. There was hymn singing in an adjoining room. As I turned to go he said, 'Let us join in prayer.' I bowed my head as he prayed for God's blessing on the stranger whose footsteps he had guided there.

THE SCHOOL OF EDUCATION

After leaving school, part of the summer holiday was spent in London with my brother. It was with relief and satisfaction, and some surprise, that a telegram arrived from my parents with the laconic message, 'Margaret Bryce £100'. This was an endowment, open only to the Liverpool Institute, provided some years previously by James Smith, wine merchant, in honour of his mother, which had supported a succession of Institute old boys at the University of Liverpool. What course to follow? Medicine and Law were considered and rejected. I was reluctant to discard the expertise in Classics, acquired with what I held to be hard labour.

Graduating with a Classics Degree in 1932, at the time of the economic depression of the 1930's, it seemed a good idea to take a one-year course for the Diploma in Education, leading to a job in teaching. I applied for admission to the Liverpool University School of Education. I was called for interview, which was taken in his study by the Professor of Education, Ernest Trafford Campagnac. By his side, as he sat in his armchair, was a many coloured parakeet on a free-standing perch. At his feet, a small dog. It was a pleasant occasion, a chat rather than an interview.

The Liverpool University School of Education

Professor Campagnac was, without intention, a tantalising figure. An Oxbridge Classics graduate, he had come to Education via His Majesty's Inspectorate. His passions were the Classics, the Renaissance, and the Cotswold area of Gloucestershire. He took us twice a week for Principles of Education. In a well-modulated voice, and, I suspect, without notes, he would speak for forty minutes on the eternal values of truth, beauty and artistic excellence. He would balance delicately the study of the humanities against the study of the sciences, to the disadvantage of the latter. He would ask how we would compare for artistic excellence the silken tapestry and the linen handkerchief, both perfect examples of the genre. Erasmus, the mediaeval Dutch scholar and humanist, was often quoted, with approval. His lectures polarised the students into those who were fascinated by his talk, and those who thought it was rubbish. But they were unanimous in the firm conviction that he could not take a class of schoolchildren. Before retirement he had ordered and supervised the building of a fine house in Cotswold stone adjacent to the church at Chipping Campden. Shortly after his retirement, we met one of his former staff in the main street. 'You must come and see the Professor' she said. I was a little reluctant, thinking that for him it might be an unwelcome chore. But we went, and were beautifully entertained to afternoon tea. The dog was still there, but not the parakeet. With the impudence of youth, I asked him why he staffed his department with people who appeared to have little experience in class teaching. He replied that he thought it was important to have people with some experience of the world.

Revisiting the School of Education in Abercromby Square in 1988, the interior was now unrecognisable after fifty-five years. An Assistant Librarian escorted me to the required section. 'I was here in the time of Professor Campagnac' I remarked, to make conversation as we passed along corridors and stairways. She said she thought she had heard the name. In the former library a bronze memorial plaque recalled —

Ernest Trafford Campagnac M.A.
Professor of Education
1908 — 1938
to whose inspiration and guidance
Abercromby House
owes so much

The History of Education was a brief introduction to the world of the Great Educators, from Plato (427-347 B.C.) to Piaget (1896-1980). The experienced teacher who has time to look back can appreciate their commitment and insight, whether it proceeded from their philosophy or, in modern times, from experience and experiment with children. Of particular interest was Jean-Jacques Rousseau (1712-1778), who maintained that the natural goodness of man was corrupted by civilised society. His book on education, Emile, (444 pages of close print in the Dent edition) was published when he was fifty, and describes in detail the recommended education for Emile from birth to his marriage and the expected arrival of his first child. A pre-arranged curriculum was out of the question. Emile was to be educated entirely through activities and by first-hand experience. 'Let him know nothing because you have told him, but because he has learnt it for himself. 'Do not ask what a child ought to know, ask what a child is capable of learning. Emile should remain in complete ignorance of those ideas which are beyond his grasp'. These sound suggestions have echoed down two centuries and formed a basis for the work of later pioneers, in particular with young children. No doubt Rousseau would have readily admitted that the pattern of his life did not match the views set out at length in Emile. As students, we maintained that few of the Great Educators could take a class, and while their relevance to primary education was agreed, we doubted their application to organised secondary education in Britain in the twentieth century.

The most valuable part of the course, in our view, was School Practice. It was taken for granted that we would all teach in Grammar Schools. We were therefore sent as students to Grammar Schools around the city for three months, and to Elementary (Council) Schools for three weeks. My elementary practice was at my first school Birchfield Road. The great hall had shrunk in size. Mr. Smith, the Principal, now approaching retirement, was still a very senior figure. But I was now taller than he, which gave me some assurance. For the first time I used a Staff Room as a member, though temporary, by right. At times the older masters looked at me, or so it seemed, with interest and compassion, as one might watch a chicken coming out of the egg, unaware of the trials which lay ahead. I was attached to a senior master. The boys, aged about ten, sat still in their fixed desks when an oral lesson was going on. After a week's observation, I was asked to give a lesson on the skin. This, my first lesson, was not a marked success. Though I had lived with it for over twenty years I knew nothing of it, and having collected a few facts from the encyclopaedia, did what I could. Afterwards my mentor kindly explained how such a lesson should be constructed. Finally a Lecturer from the School of Education came to observe and assess. The lesson was Technical Drawing. While not discouraging me, he told me that my lesson had been 'over their heads' — the pitfall of all beginners in the classroom.

Secondary teaching practice was at the Liverpool Collegiate School. This was a brother school to the Liverpool Institute, of similar age, with an imposing castellated front blackened by city grime, classrooms and furniture which, even at that time, seemed old and worn. The Staff mirrored the one I had left behind at the Institute three years ago. I was given lessons with the Upper Sixth, who were reading a book of Plato's Republic. There were some high fliers among them with Oxbridge in their sights. They clearly thought that a student from Redbrick was fair game, and tried to catch me out on points of idiom. At the Collegiate I learned much from watching experienced practitioners at work.

After Easter we returned to lectures, the preparation of a thesis, and much talk about job prospects. It was the time of the Depression of the early 1930's. Public expenditure was under attack and teachers' salaries had been cut by 10%. Previously it had been routine for an honours degree and diploma in education to qualify for a post in a grammar school, but now vacancies were few and applications unsuccessful. I spent a desultory year fielding fruitless applications, some private coaching at two shillings (10p) an hour, and half a term at Quarry Bank High School, which numbers amongst its distinguished old boys Peter Shore, the former Labour Cabinet Minister, and John Lennon of Beatles fame. As summer approached I felt I had had enough of the vain paperchase for a grammar school appointment and decided to go down market. I applied to the Liverpool Education Authority for employment as a teacher in the council schools. A reply soon arrived, regretting that there were no vacancies. There must have been a glut of well-qualified graduates at the time. Some weeks later a second letter offered an interview at the Education Office. This was the first of many sessions at the round table in the small committee room. The main committee room is an imposing essay in Victoriana, and, as the guide books say, worth a visit. A large chairman's desk and chair occupy the centre of a platform extending on each side and providing chair space for speakers. The seating, of curved benches with desk space attached, is all of polished wood — a fireman's nightmare. On occasion the platform was crowded. Some years later, during a long and boring session attended by head teachers, the Deputy Director, sitting at the end shifted his chair and fell off the platform. The audience later agreed that this had made the meeting worthwhile, and the gentleman's popularity took a marked turn for the better. The small committee room was dominated by the round table, over ten feet across. Interviewees had been heard to remark, after a gruelling session, that there were no knights at that round table. During my interview, a councillor, whose approach was less than encouraging, said 'I suppose you'll be off to a secondary school as soon as you can'. 'Not if I had given an undertaking not to', I replied. It seems this made a favourable impression and later, by post, I was offered a job, at a salary of £204 a year, including graduate allowance.

The first year of teaching was a probationary year. If service was satisfactory, and it almost always was, a certificate from the Board of Education — the title was later changed to Ministry — elevated the apprentice to tradesman status, and he or she was a qualified teacher. I was directed to Granby Street School.

THE COUNCIL SCHOOLS (2)

Granby Street was in the Toxteth area, later to become notorious for the riots of 1981. The building probably dated to the early years of the century, and perhaps before. There was no assembly hall or gymnasium. Physical education was taken in the playground, weather permitting. For assembly, the dividing screens between three classrooms were rolled back. There was no staffroom. One medium-sized room served both Head and Staff. He had his desk in one corner with chairs around the room for the Staff. There was one pedestal toilet for the men.

The staff were all two-year college trained, and it seems that my arrival caused some misgiving. It was felt that an influx of graduates might affect prospects of promotion. But I was not aware of this at the time and they were, without exception, helpful to the newcomer. The Head, Charles Ashcroft, was a gentleman. Without any of the rough edges that authority sometimes brought out, he ruled his little kingdom with a gentle hand. After assembly on the first day I returned to the Head's room, sat on one of the chairs and awaited instructions. There was much coming and going with first-day business. At morning break, the staff came in for tea and left. I was still sitting there at the end of morning school and returned at the beginning of the afternoon session. At the end of the afternoon break, the Head must have noticed that I would not go away and said I must now go along and take a lesson with class three. 'What shall I take them for?' I asked. 'History' he replied, and returned to his desk and papers. I realised that further questions would be unwelcome and found class three. I talked to them about the British Empire. Fortunately, at that time the Empire was fit and well and I was able to fill out some forty minutes. Next day I was given a timetable which provided practice with classes of all ages. I was attached to the First Assistant, as the Deputy Head was called, as guide and friend. His responsibility as Deputy Head was recognised by an additional £5 a year on his salary. It provided him, he said, with a new suit.

I was fortunate to have Arthur Midgeley as my adviser. A Yorkshireman with a war record and a passion for cricket, he had the stability and friendliness which a probationer needed. I settled into my timetable — English, arithmetic, history, geography, physical education, games. It was taken for granted that at that standard a teacher could teach anything. I began to learn the rudiments of class teaching and class management. At first, all went reasonably well. I didn't then know that it takes a class about a fortnight to get the measure of a teacher. After that he is on his own. As the weeks passed by there was a gathering cloud. For the last hour on Wednesday afternoon, I took what was called a backward class of boys aged eleven years. These were a sample of the thousands in any country who cannot cope with arithmetic, reading and spelling. It may be noticed in passing that in countries such as Germany, where spelling is completely rational and the same succession of letters always means the same sound, schoolchildren have a much easier run than with English where a host of anomalies such as 'rough' and 'bough' have to be coped with. At the beginning of the term, the Head had drawn to my attention the rules of the Education Authority regulating the use of corporal punishment. The rules were pasted in the front of the punishment book. Some of them were clearly intended as a legal safeguard for the Authority. But the general drift was sensible and humane: 'The Committee desire that, as far as possible, corporal punishment of all kinds shall be discouraged, and that discipline and good conduct in the schools shall be secured by other means.' 'No corporal punishment is to be administered otherwise than as prescribed in the following rules. All irregular forms of punishment such as boxing the ear, striking on any part of the head or shaking the body are strictly prohibited.' And so on. But the nitty gritty as far as I was concerned was the prohibition of the use of the cane during the first three years of service. Though the thinking behind this ruling was clear, it placed the young teacher at a disadvantage in a school where all the other members of the staff could use the cane if necessary. Scholars soon realised the restrictions placed upon the beginner.

My backward class was not backward in this respect. Wednesday afternoon became a time to be dreaded and by October, some were crawling up and down the gangway, urged on like racehorses by their friends seated in the desks. I decided I had had enough, that teaching was not for me, and I would go to the Head and resign. But my guardian angel intervened. At the end of one of these appalling sessions, as the class was dispersing, their teacher came in. He was the Form Master of this class, school pianist and music master. 'I see you are having trouble' he said. I managed a wan smile. 'Why don't you use the cane?' he said. 'The Head told me not to' I replied. He gave me a wink and a knowing smile. 'It's in the cupboard', he said. Next Wednesday I used it and peace was restored.

The year passed happily. Courses were followed, exams were set and marked. Games were taken at 'The Park'. In winter football and jerseys, in summer wickets, bails, bats and balls were carried nearly a mile down to Sefton Park. At the end of the games period the equipment was distributed to the boys who took it home and returned it to school the next day. The school fielded two or three teams each season, which played inter-school matches on a Saturday morning. Not surprisingly, considering the enthusiasm of Arthur Midgeley, the cricket teams were hard to beat. He organised the summer camp at Braithwaite in the Lake District. It is there that I last remember him. We were sitting together on the hillside overlooking the camp ground, where a game of cricket was in progress. The boy at the wicket was one whose character, at that early age, showed courage and friendliness. 'He's the sort of boy you would like to have for your own' he remarked. I wondered whether he was without a family.

Arthur even forgave me for joining the National Union of Teachers. The NUT was, and still is, the largest teachers' Union. During the first half of the century its membership had a majority of single women teachers. It seems that men teachers, returning from war service in World War I, some of them in the appalling conditions of trench warfare, had a strong sense of grievance about measures which had been taken by the NUT in their absence. They formed a breakaway Union, the National Association of Schoolmasters, now the National Association of Schoolmasters and Union of Women Teachers. The NUT and the NAS were always at loggerheads. Until 1955 women teachers' pay was about four fifths of the equivalent men teachers' pay. This, no doubt, was meant to recognise the man teacher's domestic responsibilities. Nevertheless, the women demanded equal pay for equal work, while the men demanded separate consideration. In 1955 the first stage of giving equal pay to women teachers began. It was to be spread over a period of seven years. The movement of women towards employment and independence took the edge off this dispute, but the division remained.

Summer camp ended my probationary period at Granby Street. I had been given every help and encouragement. It was customary for the exprobationer now to seek a permanent appointment. After a few weeks filling a temporary vacancy at another school, I was called for interview at Heyworth Street Council School. It was not a sought-after appointment and there was only one other candidate. On the interviewing panel as a rule there was a Schools Inspector from the Liverpool Education Office. These Inspectors, few in number, were not to be confused with His Majesty's Inspectors, who were appointed nationally by the Ministry, then the Board of Education. Usually they were appointed from Liverpool Head Teachers who had made a favourable impression. After a few routine questions, he asked me whether I thought I could 'hold the job down'. The implication was that this down-town school might be a testing ground for a young teacher. Having been in the job market for a year, I mentally crossed my fingers and said 'Yes'.

Heyworth Street, in the Everton district, was of an age with Granby Street, though it had a small staff room and a gymnasium in the basement. There was poverty in the area. On the way to school one would meet boys who had been sent out by their mothers to the grocers to buy two pennyworth of margarine for the breakfast. The Head Master, Joseph Emblen, while shrewd and capable, deserves a place in the comedy of education. The assembly was taken in three adjoining rooms with the screens pushed back. On the first morning a colleague, an acquaintance from University days, whispered, 'Get ready for a pantomime'. The Head came in at the far end, walking aggressively with arms swinging. Reaching his position, he shouted an order which, it later transpired, was 'Shake yourselves up out of it'. At this, some three hundred boys rose from their seats, bent their arms, closed their fists, and waved them about. Humorists, out of sight of the Head, would turn to face each other in shadow boxing. At a second order they would resume their seats. This was intended to make the boys alert and attentive. It is hard to believe in retrospect that this took place, as it did, in a singing lesson. During the singing of 'Drink to me only with thine eyes' the order would be given, the arms would jerk to and fro, and on command the boys would resume their seats and the song would continue.

Then there was the Annual Prizegiving. At mid-morning the school was assembled. At the front was a trestle table with a small pile of books. Joe would enter, take up his position, and bark. The school rose with arms flailing. Probably he would have liked to have had the Staff doing it as well. Another bark and they sat down. He would point to a boy 'You, do you see any councillors here?' 'No sir' the lad would reply dutifully. He pointed to another boy 'Do you see any inspectors here?' 'No sir', he replied, with such conviction as to imply that anyone who did see an inspector present was a fool. 'Neither do I' Joe went on. He continued 'I had a letter the other day from the Education Office asking me to tell them when our prizegiving would be, so that councillors and inspectors could attend.

But I don't see any'. Having made his point he turned to the table and in five minutes, without comment, handed out the books and the school dispersed.

My timetable was basic, and I was not called upon to do anything beyond my inexperience. At that time, before inflation, children were encouraged to save. On Monday morning they brought their pennies which were entered on their cards, and the money was taken by the caretaker to the nearest branch of the Liverpool Savings Bank, whose pass books were fronted with the advice 'If you wish to rise in life, begin to save'. I was put on the ledger and learned to add up a column of figures, a facility which surprises the youngsters of today.

A three-year stint at Heyworth Street was good grounding in classroom competence — adequate preparation, the importance of punctuality to school or class — the unpunctual teacher finds a restless class which has been a distraction to nearby colleagues before he arrives — in front of the class deliberate and clear speech in language they can understand, avoiding long words and abstract nouns, knowledge to be imparted in digestible quantities regardless of the distance covered (external examinations were not in prospect), skills (crafts, gymnastics) to be split into their component parts, taught separately over a period, then gathered into a whole. These unexciting teacher virtues, although, alas, not always adhered to, were identified as the signposts to success. After three years' apprenticeship it seemed time to look for another school. In 1938 applications were invited for two schools, Sefton Park adapted, and Dingle Vale purpose built, to comply with 'Hadow Recommendations'. The Hadow Report, issued in 1926, taking its name from its Chairman, was the forerunner of a series of Reports on educational issues, interrupted by the war, and then continuing into the 1960's. A group of people, eminent in Education and other relevant professions, was invited by the government to consider, examine, and recommend on 'the organisation, objective, and curriculum of courses of study suitable for children who will remain in full time attendance at schools other than Secondary (Grammar) Schools, up to the age of fifteen, regard being had on the one hand to the requirements of a good general education and the desirability of providing a reasonable variety of curriculum, so far as is possible, for children of varying tastes and abilities, and on the other hand to the probable occupation of the pupils in commerce, industry, and agriculture.' This foreshadowed the end of the old elementary schools organised in classes from Standard 1 to Standard 7. Primary education would finish at 11 plus. Secondary education would be established in its own right for children between the ages of 11 to 14 (to be raised later to 15 and 16) in schools which would provide for differing abilities and requirements.

The Report, approved by the government, went to the Board of Education for implementation. In

Liverpool the Report of the Education Committee for 1932/3 reacted with less than enthusiasm. — 'From communications received from the Board of Education the Sub-committee have learnt that the Board still regard the Authority as under the obligation to further some of the objects to which attention was drawn in an earlier Circular, viz. the general reorganisation of the Elementary Schools into departments on the lines of the Hadow Report.'

I was fortunate to be appointed to Sefton Park School a deciding factor being my willingness to play the piano for assembly. Sefton Park had started life as the Holt Secondary (Grammar) School, later transferred to a fine building on Queen's Drive, Liverpool's ring road. An assembly hall, gymnasium, woodwork rooms and a laboratory had been equipped from existing accommodation. A small fifth form of voluntary "stayers-on" was provided for.

The year at Sefton Park was a new dimension. The newly-formed schools had attracted many applications for the teaching posts. Most of the appointed staff, all men, became Heads in due course. Packed lunches (school meals were not generally available) were taken in the mid-day break and the conversation round the staff room table on school, education and the problems of home gardening, was an unexpected bonus. But I was disappointed that the conversation rarely turned to Europe. Adolf Hitler, whose name had appeared in the newspapers with increasing regularity during the past decade, at first presented as a comic figure with a Charlie Chaplin moustache, was now the German Head of State. Austria had been annexed and the Sudetenland district of Czechoslovakia had been ceded to Germany by the Munich Agreement, which was to be the downfall of the Prime Minister Neville Chamberlain.

Here I had a special interest, having spent the New Year of 1934/5 in Cologne. Having learnt a little German I wanted to find out if what had been learnt in text books found a response in the country of origin. As the train from Ostend crossed the frontier at Aachen, one was aware of the sharp transition from the lackadaisical to the efficient. Frau Goossens met me at Cologne station and took me to their apartment in the Trajanstrasse. She apologised that there was a bed in the sitting room, but pointed out that she was old enough to be my grandmother. I sat at meals with the family — father, mother and sons. The male members of the family did not speak to me, not from animosity, but they appeared to think that I was mother's business. The Nazi flags were flying from public buildings and houses. When the family was out she would talk freely. She would make fun of the brisk commands on the Party parades transmitted on the radio. Hitler had been Chancellor for less than a year, and when asked, she said that the Revolution was strongest in Bavaria and had not affected the Rheinland so much. She recalled the runaway inflation of the early 1920's and got out her housekeeping records. These were kept in a large ledger on a free-standing desk. She turned the pages to show the price rise in succeeding weeks of a box of matches - 1 mark - 10 marks - 50 marks - 100 marks - 1,000 marks - 10,000 marks. "What happened?" I asked. "They said, 'From now a million marks shall be one mark' ", she replied. Bank balances, public or private, immediately lost all value. It was clear that this catastrophe was due to the impossible burden of reparations imposed on the Germans after the First World War, and that Hitler and his party had been the only ones to stand up to the ex-Allies, and as they said, "shake off the fetters of the Treaty of Versailles." He had restored to the German nation their self-respect.

Some five and a half years later, Hitler's stranglehold on the German people and his lust for power caused us to assemble at school on the morning of 3rd September 1939. There were no lessons. Our job was to fit the boys with gas masks and escort them to the evacuation area. At eleven o'clock the wireless sets were turned on, and the sad voice of the Prime Minister informed us that Poland had been invaded and that Britain was now at war with Germany. We took the train from Liverpool to Broxton, south of Chester, and from there by coach and car to our destination, the village of Farndon.

Farndon is on the edge of England. Its bridge over the River Dee leads into Holt, in Wales. Brought up in a suburb, the village struck an immediate chord - the countryside, the gardens, the quietness, the sense of community. I felt I could stay for ever. Later, we were to be aware of rank and precedence. The writ of the Duke of Westminster ran through the villages. His headquarters, and sometime residence, was Eaton Hall, to be seen across the fields from the Chester to Farndon road, its clock-tower a lookalike of Big Ben. The Duke was the summit. Then the county families, sometimes a military rank at the head. Then the bourgeoisie — the well-to-do farmers, untouched by the hardships of wartime rationing, the vicar, the doctor, the schoolmaster perhaps, the tradespeople perhaps. Then the labourers. On social occasions it was not done to break ranks - farmers' wives would only invite farmers' children to their parties.

Into this feudal and conservative society we were an unfamiliar and unwelcome intrusion. It is to the credit of both sides that we lived amicably together as long as it took. From the train we were taken to the village hall where the proceedings were a free for all. Realising that we must look after ourselves, I went up to a gentleman who was sitting by himself "Do you want some guests?" I asks hesitantly. "No, we don't", he replied with a weary smile, "but we have to". We went off together, and were looked after well, until we found a family who were more interested.

Our job was two-fold - to see that our charges were properly housed and to take some lessons in the village school when there was room; there were too many of us to be absorbed into the local classes. It was fine September weather and the fruit was on the trees, ripe for picking. The city boys thought it was waiting for them, to the amusement of their village friends. We noted with some envy how well-behaved and obedient the local youngsters were in class.

Visiting staff had an insight into the workload of a big farm, sometimes carrying over two hundred head of cattle. The domestic and farm buildings of the area were well built and commodious, presenting a typical facade of patterned brick and white stucco gables. Some of the farm kitchens were as big as a small hall, with furniture and fittings to match. The women had little time to spare and indeed the men also, of whom we saw little.

On the first two weekends there was an influx of visiting parents in holiday mood. But as the weeks passed without enemy action, a drift back to the city began, and as autumn gave way to winter, visitors were few.

In the village society the Rector was the most important person. He was very involved in the school and personally took charge of preparing the children for the Christmas concert. He explained to me that the difference between his incumbency and that of his non-conformist colleagues was security of tenure. He seemed to feel that they were something of a poor relation. I heard that the church at the village of Shocklach, some five miles away, had a Saxon arch. Access was by the incumbent's permission. I found myself back in the nineteenth century. The house near the church seemed isolated. His room, full of paraphernalia, recalled the Old Curiosity Shop. He took me into the tiny church and pointed out the arch over the altar and got out the church register, where in earlier times, notes had been made of useful recipes. Perhaps writing paper had been expensive and hard to come by. I was told later that the Shocklach living was in the gift of two sisters living in neighbouring Crewe Hall.

Apart from being away from home, the time passed pleasantly enough for the staff. The teaching load was light, though visiting in winter required a good overcoat and wellington boots. It was the severe winter of 1939/40 and we were snowed up. There was no transport to and from the village for a fortnight. The Head, travelling from Liverpool, had to walk eight miles from Chester through the snow. While we admired his hardihood, being the Head, he had no sympathy.

Before the days of central heating, the temperature in the village bedrooms was arctic. Our house was sure of its water supply from a pump in the back yard. It had served the household as far back as they could remember, but when I used it, it broke. I was regarded with misgiving, if not suspicion, until the expert from a neighbouring village announced that a copper ring had succumbed to the passage of time. Still, I felt it had waited for me.

There was a cinema with performances given if there was an audience. One evening we turned up unannounced, and the film "The Mikado" was put on for our sole benefit. Or one could go to the village institute and play billiards or attend the occasional whist drive. The farm people thought we were a lazy lot and, indeed, beyond part-time teaching and visiting there was little else to do. With the movement back of boys to their families in Liverpool, a corresponding number of teachers returned and we were instructed to report back at Sefton Park school each morning for home teaching. In war-time Liverpool it was like moving from an oasis to a desert.

Home teaching was an effort to keep alive the basic subjects in the homes of willing parents, but it was a makeshift business. Attendance could not be insisted upon and there was, not surprisingly, when the previous night might have been spent in an air-raid shelter, little inclination to work.

For the war had come to our cities. The Battle of Britain during the late summer of 1940 was followed by night raids. Liverpool had its share, culminating in the eight-day blitz of May 1941. I was reporting each night for duty in the Auxiliary Fire Service. On the way to the Fire Station in Heswall, I would get off my motor bike at the top of Pensby Hill and look back on the line of fire from the Liverpool docks. At the end of the eight days I felt the exhaustion which was the common experience of many at that time. The morning journey from the Wirral was by underground or by boat across the Mersey. Emerging from James Street station the city centre was silent, no buses, cars or transport of any kind. The only sound, the padding of footsteps picking their way through the rubble to the office, or its debris.

I had now been moved to Anfield Road School, a large building of the red-brick era, comprising four departments of boys and girls. The Headmaster, Alec Eaves, had business interests and a wider experience than most of us. Among the staff there was an unusual knowledge of practical skills. One master was able to put a clock back together again, having taken it apart and repaired it. He was skilled in knotting and splicing and demonstrated elaborate examples of the art. Another was an accomplished pianist and organist, and spoke convincingly about workshop machine tools. On Open Day the Science Master set out an intricate display which flashed and buzzed when activated. There was fire-watching duty at night. Camp-beds were provided, and stirrup pumps and buckets of sand to deal with incendiary bombs. It was an eerie business patrolling in the darkness unaccompanied through long corridors, the silence broken by the occasional fire of a mobile anti-aircraft gun outside or the drone of enemy planes above on their way to Manchester or Belfast.

This brief period was terminated by being called up to the National Fire Service. Prior to this, I had attended another school of quite a different kind. Heswall friends, members of the local sailing club, were preparing for a Yacht Masters Coastal Certificate, which would qualify for officer rank in the R.N.V.R. on the Royal Navy's light craft. The

Liverpool Nautical College was the sole property and occupation of Captain Roberts in his retirement. We went after work to his room in the city. He knew everything about seamanship, though not expert in explaining it. The examinations were held in the old Liverpool Custom House near the Pier Head. An eye test for sight and colour, the Compass, Navigation, Meteorology, and an interview to test practical knowledge.. With few candidates, the papers were marked right away, and failing in one of them was considered to be failure in the whole exam, and the candidate was discharged. The interview took place in a room which appeared full of mahogany furniture and brass apparatus. The interviewing officer matched the room, with mahogany complexion and gold-braided uniform. "So you want to command a small boat, Mr Bridge", he began. In my nervousness he seemed to suggest that this was an amusing, if not dangerous, idea. My inexperience was soon found out - I had been out on the Mersey and the Dee three or four times. "You'd better come back in six months' time", he said, concluding the interview with a smile.

My three and a half years as a fireman made me a better teacher. I had learnt a new trade, and become aware of the discipline of physical work and a craft well learnt and well carried out. I had been one of a team of working men, experienced at first hand their character and abilities, and came to understand the disadvantages of the limitation of educational opportunity in early years. The NFS was a correction to the monastic aspect of school teaching - from primary school to secondary school, to university or college of education, and back to school. Later, a school governor was to tell me "Teachers don't know how the world ticks". Perhaps in the 1990's this is not the case. But there is little doubt that a year or two in commerce or industry could well be recognised as a desirable element of teacher training.

THE SECONDARY MODERN SCHOOLS

I was among the first returners to the Liverpool teaching service. Those from the armed forces were to come later. Though I was still formally on the staff of Sefton Park School, I was directed to Earle Road School in the Edge Hill district. As far as the building was concerned this was back to square one. No assembly hall, though there was a woodwork room and a nearby temporary building doubled as a gymnasium and a dining room.

His name revealed that the Head Master, Dai Jones, was a Welshman. He was one of many Welsh schoolteachers in the city. Liverpool was sometimes referred to at that time as 'the capital of North Wales'. From the small towns as far south as Llandudno and Wrexham, its citizens would come on their closing day - Thursday - to shop in the big department stores. Traditionally the Welsh have cared for education and they contributed an effective minority to the Liverpool teaching force. Dai Jones was beginning his Headship, and was no doubt looking forward to the return of men teachers from the Forces - the school was all boys - and the easing of wartime restrictions.

I was given the backward class. The classroom was not an inspiring workplace. Old furniture, interior needing decoration, and windows, uncleaned on the outside since the beginning of the war, carrying five years accumulated grime. As a retired fireman I had no doubt what to do. Taking half a dozen boys down to the cellar, we found a ladder, some buckets of water, and a stirrup pump which had survived wartime use, and headed for the street outside the classroom. As this procession crossed the playground the Head came to the door. 'What's going on?' he shouted. 'Cleaning the windows, sir,' I replied, keeping moving in case he wanted to intervene. Before he could decide what to do we were round the corner, the ladder was erected, and the boys below appreciating a new dimension in post-war education, pumped heartily, while at the top I felt that skills acquired in wartime had an unexpected relevance to peace-time reconstruction.

It was soon clear that the class of 12/13 year old boys would not respond to a conventional time-table, and the last hour of each day - when in all schools the output on both sides of the teacher's desk is slowing down - was occupied with 'activities'. Simple models were planned and made from wood, cardboard, and paper. Netting, requiring only a netting needle, a drawing pin stuck in the desk, and string, gave those who could use their fingers the chance to produce squares, bags, and finally a hammock. This gained general approval except from the man in the next room who had to put up with the racket. I was still, by appointment, on the staff of Sefton Park School, better equipped and more sought-after than Earle Road. But Dai Jones indicated that he would be glad for me to stay. After a war-time love affair, I was now living on my own. Perhaps he felt I needed looking after. I decided to stay and was allowed to do so without interview or formalities.

At Earle Road I began to feel that I was not a beginner. Class teaching had become routine and, apart from preparation, required no effort. I looked for ways to occupy spare time, and got together a school concert. Summer camps for the boys were starting up again and under the guidance of the Head, I had a go at the organisation. Bell tents were dormitories for staff and boys - eight boys to a tent on ground sheets and blankets. Three staff to a tent on camp beds. These, with a small marquee (staff) and a big marquee (boys) for meals, were hired and transported to the favourite destination, the Isle of Man. A grant from the Education Authority reduced the charge for the boys to a pittance, paid in advance by small instalments. For the staff who took part it was a voluntary service, perhaps an acknowledgement of the longer holidays which are part of the teacher's contract.

We soon learned the hazards of the first night. Eight boys together in the dark, sixteen feet around the base of the tent pole, the novelty, the excitement and the anonymity. Patrolling staff outside a tent in the dark might overhear a critical appraisal of their character. Sleep at last, but at 4.00 a.m. they were out on the field playing cricket. Later we tried taking them out for a long walk before retiring - to little effect. The second night and thereafter sleep was unbroken.

Summer Camps, especially those for the under-privileged, are a recurring theme in the Education Committee's Annual Reports. In 1932/3 102 camps were held at a cost in grants of £1,757. 'So great was the demand for assistance that the grants had to be reduced to 12s 6d (62½p) per leader and eight shillings (40p) per child. The total cost of the camps this year was £5,491'. Thirty years later in 1962/3 126 parties at home and 74 abroad were assisted by grants totalling £8,600. The summer camps under canvas became an institution in boys' schools, though some opted to use sheltered accommodation. They were a boon to parents hard put to make ends meet, and an educational bonus - a bond was set up, not possible in school surroundings, between staff and boys, who discovered their teachers as human beings, sharing the same food and accommodation and working on their behalf.

At this time mid-day meals became widely available in schools. Since the 1920's Education Authorities had had to deal with the effects of poverty evident in children attending school. In 1929 the Liverpool City Council made a grant of £250 'for the purchase of clogs and rubber-soled shoes for the supply of footwear for use by children arriving at school with wet feet'. Undernourishment meant inability to cope with school, and 'free dinners for necessitous children' continued to be provided on week-days during school terms and holidays. The hardships of war-time highlighted this need, and the Butler Education Act of 1944 required LEA's to provide milk and meals for pupils in maintained schools. (The supply of free milk to secondary schools was stopped in 1968.) This was a boon for working mothers who were still housekeeping within the limits of food rationing, which continued for a time after the war. The Local Authorities then organised the supply and delivery of mid-day meals, prepared either in central kitchens, or occasionally, at that time, on school premises. The schools, in turn, were instructed to arrange the necessary accommodation in the assembly hall if there was one. If not, outside premises were rented.

The case for school meals lost some, but not all of its force during the succeeding decades. It was good for young people to have a substantial meal each day, and a well-planned diet, with beneficial effects to health and growth. Not all parents could be relied on to do this. A well organised and supervised mealtime sets a standard for later years, and may be considered part of the education process. Is the expense justified? In the year 1984/5 school meals and milk cost the taxpayer £527 million. It may be noticed that a number of scholars, instead of taking a nourishing meal in school, preferred to go out of the building and buy chips, buns, and cakes.

There was controversy and ill-feeling over supervision. The teachers were given to understand that, under legislation, it was compulsory, and the Unions did not contest it. What about teachers who went out of school at mid-day as they were entitled to do? What about recompense for the arduous duty done after a morning in the classroom, either by payment or an increase in off-duty time? The teachers were reluctant to press the issue, the authorities were happy to be relieved of a problem, and the unsatisfactory arrangement lasted for over two decades.

There was now an opportunity to take my class for a fortnight into the country. Colomendy Camp School in North Wales had been opened by the Liverpool Education Committee in 1940. Beautifully situated in a fold of the hills near the Loggerheads Inn between Mold and Ruthin, the timber buildings were purpose built, providing space for teaching and recreation, and for dormitories, at each end of which was a staff cubicle. The big house was the Head's residence and administration block. Presented at first by enthusiasts as offering a public school education to the so-called working class, its growth had been halted by war-time restrictions. It was in business again, and in May 1947 we travelled by Liverpool Corporation bus to gain a nodding acquaintance with country life, not then easily available to city boys. A farm, the nearby villages, and the market town of Mold were visited. For maths we measured the width of the river by triangulation. For

A class of Earle Road Boys at the Colomendy Camp School

geography we checked that the surrounding hills had been correctly placed on the Ordnance Survey On walks the boys were taught country manners - the proper disposal of litter, the closing of field gates, and generally respect and understanding, as far as they were able, for another way of life. The resident staff were co-operative. One of them, called 'The Major' from his military background, offered to help me in 'getting them up in the morning'. I was not aware that this would be a problem, but, bowing to experience, I agreed. He occupied the staff cubicle at the other end of the dormitory. At 7.00 a.m. he emerged in dressing gown and towel. 'Get up', he roared in regimental fortissimo. I remembered the story of the Duke of Wellington and the drill sergeant - 'By God, if he didn't frighten them, he frightened me.' The boys dropped out of bed en masse and looked at me. I felt I had betrayed them. 'Get your toilet bags' he shouted, and led us all to the ablutions.

The early promise as a non-fee-paying public school did not stand the test of time. Parents were not by tradition committed to the idea of their children being away from home, and the resident school population came and went. It was clear that the style of education which had evolved for one social class could not be transplanted successfully on to another. But over the years it fully justified its place in Liverpool's education service. It provided residential education for those who wanted it, an International Camp in the summer attended by parties from abroad, and many projects by visiting groups to supplement courses in geology, geography, biology and botany. In the late 1960's a permanent building was erected on the site, providing 150 residential places for boys and girls, allowing the existing accommodation to be used exclusively for visiting parties.

Impossible in war-time, music festivals were starting up again. They were massed choirs of some 200/300 boys and girls from the schools of a district. A programme was drawn up at the beginning of the autumn term, to be learnt in school ready for rehearsals in the spring. Performances were in the new Philharmonic Hall. The old Philharmonic had been destroyed by fire before the war. There I had heard Rachmaninov play, a tall, drooping figure who seemed to me very old. Nevertheless, after a full programme, he played three encores of the Prelude in C sharp minor.

In addition to preparing my boys for the festival, I was not smart enough to avoid becoming responsible for movement control. This was to arrange the passage of the contributing choirs through cloakroom accommodation where they left their overcoats, and on to the platform where I had arranged the seating. The dress rehearsal provided a dummy run. I confess that on the night I was gratified, and at first thrilled, to see them all in their places as had been planned. The performances were inspiring occasions. The auditorium was usually full. Before the War the conductor had been one of the school music masters. Now, at the Education Office, there was a

Music Adviser, who took his rightful place on the rostrum. Under his baton the boys and girls sang with gusto. What they lacked in art they made up in spontaneity.

At the Festivals, I was fortunate to make the acquaintance of Dr. Caleb Jarvis. A professional organist and teacher of the organ, well-known to Liverpool audiences, he was impatient of affectation and pretence. We stood together in the wings during the interval while the new Director of Education was making a speech, at our request, to fill the gap. Caleb turned to me and remarked, "Blah, blah, blah." "I take it you refer to the Director of Education", I observed with heavy humour. "Blah, blah, blah", he replied. He could make the organ speak. A favourite finale was Bach's "Sheep May Safely Graze". Having the run of the rooms and stairways behind the sides of the platform, I found a viewpoint surrounded by organ pipes. The small figure at the console down below was incredibly the source of the majestic clamour which surrounded me.

Towards the end of three years at Earle Road - I was now taking classes of normal ability range - thoughts turned to promotion. I was now thirty-six. I sounded the Head. "Carry on," he said. After one or two attempts I was shortlisted for the post of Deputy Head of Florence Melly Secondary Modern Boys School in the Clubmoor district. At that time there was no extra pay for the Deputy of a small school of two hundred plus. The position was also temporary in the absence of the holder as Lecturer at an Emergency Training College. We candidates, waiting outside the interview room at the Education Office, agreed that it was not much of a job. I was appointed.

The idea of secondary schools for non-academic children can trace its conception to the Hadow Report of 1926 and its birth to the Norwood Report of 1943. The Norwood Committee was charged with the duty 'to consider suggested changes in the secondary school curriculum and the question of school examinations in relation thereto.' It began by suggesting that schoolchildren should be divided into three types. 'There is first the pupil who is interested in learning for its own sake, who can grasp an argument or follow a piece of connected reasoning. Secondly the pupils whose abilities lie markedly in the field of applied science or applied art. And finally the type of pupil who deals more easily with concrete things than ideas.' For the first type there would be the secondary grammar school, for the second the secondary technical school, for the third the secondary modern school. This classification of youngsters took up ideas advanced in previous Reports. Subsequent experience suggested that it was not an accurate account of the range and difference of the abilities of schoolchildren.

Most teachers would have agreed - and it was confirmed by examination results - that roughly twenty-five per cent of the school population were capable of following an academic curriculum, whether it was in the arts or sciences or a mixture of both. What of the other seventy-five per cent who could compete on equal terms in art, woodwork, metalwork, light crafts, housecraft, physical education, music, games, and outdoor pursuits? Were they to be written off as the also-rans? Indeed no, said the Reports, emphasising that their schools must have 'parity of status'. And in fact when post-war shortages ceased to bite, Education Authorities up and down the country did what they could to provide modern, well-equipped buildings for the secondary modern school.

The title 'modern' is a teasing description, and its provenance may intrigue the researcher. The members of the Norwood and earlier Committees had no difficulty in describing the schools for the literary and scientific bright - grammar, and for the so-called technical bright - technical. But a suitable description of the rest, without causing an uproar? Perhaps the inspiration which produced "modern" received discreetly in due course the appropriate recognition. At first it was thought by the interested public that the new secondary modern schools would operate a new and effective education technique bringing them into line with the grammar schools. It soon became clear that the grammar and technical schools were the way to the professions and careers of equal status, and that pupils from the modern schools would generally proceed, with varying success according to their work potential, character and personality, to the many essential occupations of contemporary society. Parental ambition and educational snobbery ensured that in public estimation the secondary modern schools soon took third place.

Nevertheless, those who taught in the secondary modern schools from their beginning shortly after the War until the comprehensive reorganisation in the 1960's, can testify to the excellent pioneering work that was done in them. Free until the late 1950's from the pressure of external examinations, courses were fitted to the pupils' abilities and interests. Where appropriate, instruction was organised round a centre of interest - e.g. Transport through Time - which provided material for research, and written, spoken and artistic exercises in History, Geography, Applied Science and Art. Starting from an initial survey and organisation of the programme to be covered, the project ended with an impressive display of their work, which other classes were invited to inspect. Throughout, there was a stimulating atmosphere of freedom and experiment, in contrast to earlier formal procedures. It made heavy demands on their initiative and ability to work unsupervised, and indeed, when it was all over they were glad to get back to some old-fashioned class teaching for a while.

This atmosphere was fostered by the promise of the 1944 Education Act, identified by name with R.A. Butler, then President of the Board of Education. It was brought to the statute book through the customary stages of proposal and consultation, without political dissension, during the hard years of World War II. Perhaps it is not a coincidence that previous Education Acts - 1902, 1918, - were also passed when the country was at war. The 1944 Act laid on Local Education Authorities the duty to secure adequate provision of primary and secondary schools in their area. They were required to submit a plan for organisation in three successive stages — primary, secondary and further, - in separate institutions. The LEA's were urged to contribute towards the spiritual, moral, mental and physical development of the community by ensuring efficient education throughout these stages. In the schools we felt that in intention at least the Government was on our side.

Florence Melly School was named after a lady who had given voluntary service to Liverpool schools over a number of years. It was said that, in the more deferential period before the war, when visiting a school, she would make her presence known to the Head Master on the floor above by banging her stick on the stair banisters below. George Melly, of the Footwarmers and TV art programmes, is, as he might agree, an untypical member of the family. The naming of schools after individuals was open to question. At the time it seems an appropriate and well-deserved recognition of meritorious service. But the building outlasts sentiment and the association loses relevance. In this case the name lent itself too readily to schoolboy humour.

Schools similar in design to Florence Melly had already attracted attention, at home and abroad, as 'open air' schools. This referred to the position of the classrooms, woodwork room, laboratory, and ancillary rooms round two grassed quadrangles, separated by the assembly hall/gymnasium. Movement between the rooms was along open verandahs. Land was not in short supply and the playing field adjoined the building. The architects, under the direction of the Education Authority, had successfully expressed in bricks and mortar the intention of the Hadow Report that there should be parity of status between all secondary schools. It was a pleasure to work in.

The Head Master, W.S. Buckley, was in the right job. An English specialist, and the author of school text books on the subject, he had the knowledge and experience to guide a younger staff. Due to the effect of the War on the recruitment of men teachers into the profession, there was an age gap between the Head and the rest of us. Some were entrants through the Emergency Training Colleges, established as a temporary measure to bring in ex-service men after one year's training.

It was here that for the first time in teaching I was clothed in a little brief authority. At the age of thirty-nine I felt I had the experience and seniority for initiative. Fortunately the Staff included new entrants whose enthusiasm had not been tempered by time. The Head soon gave us a free rein. There was already a summer camp in covered accommodation. We considered that a canvas camp would bring more out of the boys, and decided to find a new site on the west coast of the Isle of Man.

Summer Camp. The author announces the orders of the day

During half-term at the end of February I went to the fishing town of Peel to explore. The scene, as I turned into the south end of the promenade, was one of winter and emptiness, grey skies, a grey sea stirred by the wind and, as far as I could see, not a person in sight. I was the only guest in a fair-sized hotel. On the first evening the proprietor took his meal with me. For the remaining time I dined alone. It transpired later that he had reason to be suspicious of a solitary guest in winter.

Enquiries led to Ballawyllin Farm, about a mile inland on the road to Tynwald Hill and Douglas. Mr Boyde was to be our friend for as long as we wanted him. The rent was insignificant. The field he found for us was excellent - level, dry, with access to the road. A cooking range was needed. By good fortune there were still available some ranges made for emergency use in the city streets after air raids during the War. Five pounds secured one. No doubt, either whole or in parts, it is still somewhere on the island. In five years of the Ballawyllin camps a scene stays in the memory. One of the boys was a dwarf, his legs half normal length. To keep up with his friends he had to move his legs twice as fast, and necessity had enabled him to do so without effort. On a hot July morning a group had been into Peel and were walking back at midday. As they neared camp we saw that the others had found short tree branches in leaf and were holding them over his head to provide shade while they walked and he scuttled along together, they without a smile and he without self-consciousness or concern. I wondered

Summer Camp Ballawyllin Farm, Peel, Isle of Man

Summer Camp in the Isle of Man. Some staff carry their badges of office.

how deep was the origin of this untaught care for the disabled.

At this time both the telephone and a part-time Secretary made their appearance in the Secondary Modern Schools. The Head, who had managed happily without them for most of his professional life, seemed uncertain what to do with either. The Secretary was given work in the library, and incoming calls obliged him to accept the telephone.

As in most schools, students on teaching practice came and went. The Federation of Malaya, now enlarged and re-named Malaysia, was in 1952 a Crown Colony. The British Government agreed to a request from Malaysia to help to establish a teacher base. With the cooperation of the Liverpool education service the Malayan Teachers Training College was established at Kirkby on the city's outskirts. In school the Malayan students were a welcome novelty. Fluent English speakers, they told us about their country, stressing the importance of the Indians and the Chinese in their society. We should not refer to the students as Malays - these were the labouring classes.

They invited us to their dances and I saw for the first time the beauty of many coloured dresses against dark skin. One of our students, an Indian, wore a light coloured sharkskin jacket with his evening dress. I complimented him on his turn-out. "It doesn't seem to attract the girl I want", he muttered despondently. A Japanese girl, who must

Florence Melly Boys' School Staff with the Malayan students

have been shorter than five feet, with faultless complexion and exquisite dress, resembled a finely fashioned doll. "Where are you going to teach?" we asked. "After I have qualified, I shall go home" she replied, "to be married." We asked about her fiance. She told us a little, and added, "But I haven't seen him yet," explaining that in Japan it was part of parental duty to choose a bridegroom. We said that no doubt she knew that in Britain couples chose each other. "Yes", she said, "but I think my parents are able to choose better than I can."

It was at Florence Melly that I had my first and only experience of a full-scale inspection by His Majesty's Inspectors. His (now Her) Majesty's Inspectors of Schools are a venerable institution with a noteworthy record of a high standard of public service. At the end of the decade which saw the Reform Act of 1832, a Committee of the Privy Council was set up "for the consideration of all matters affecting the education of the people" and "to superintend the application of any sums voted by Parliament for the purpose of promoting public education." The Committee made government inspection a condition of financial aid. Two Inspectors were appointed by the Archbishops of the Church of England, who would report both on the teaching of religion and of secular subjects. The Inspectors, however, were not to interfere with the teaching and administration of a school. Thus the Inspectorate was founded, as a watchdog for public expenditure and efficiency.

The relationship between HMI's and teachers was not always a happy one. In 1860, under the influence of the current economic dogma of value for money, government grants to education became dependent on pupils' attendance and examination results. A feeling of mutual distrust arose between the Inspectors who had to examine the children and the teachers whose livelihood depended on their reports. It took four decades to recognise the damage done by "payment by results" - excessive pressure on the children and attempts to massage records of attendance and to produce the appearance of results by devious means.

The most famous HMI was Matthew Arnold, eldest son of Thomas Arnold, eminent Headmaster of Rugby School in the earlier part of the last century. In a hard-working life, Matthew successfully combined the duties of an HMI for 35 years, with literary excellence in some forty works of poetry and prose. As an HMI he was sent abroad to examine the state of education in France, Germany and Holland. He contrasted English secondary schools of the time unfavourably with those he saw on the Continent and recommended action by the Government to establish a state system of secondary education in England to make good the deficiencies of the existing system sponsored by the churches. By a programme of inspection based on priorities they provided the Government with the information needed to guide policy and plan ahead. They offered advice to schools, either directly or through teachers' courses, publications and liaison with local education offices. They had no executive powers.

For the younger teacher, to be inspected was an uneasy experience. Prior notice was given, and during the run-up, sins of omission, disregarded in more carefree times, began to loom large. Displays of work and other exhibits appeared in the classrooms. Records were updated. Notes of courses attended were rescued, dusted off, and revised. All to no avail. The Inspectors, like visiting royalty, were well aware of these cosmetic procedures. The experienced teacher didn't bother. The Inspectors, well-qualified in their speciality and articulate, with the advantage of access to all schools in their area and elsewhere (they were expected to accept transfer to another district once or twice in their career) had little difficulty in impressing their authority upon the class teacher, albeit with much courtesy. He or she, in their turn, felt that the Inspector had little of immediate help to offer the teacher in the classroom, and I must confess that this was my experience. HMI's no doubt would feel that their duties had a wider reference.

After the inspection, which lasted three or four days, there was a printed report which offered a detailed assessment of courses and method, and which noticed strengths and weaknesses. It was couched in elegant prose of which Macaulay would not have been ashamed. Faults were finely graded, causing, in ascending order, concern, misgiving, disquiet and, in really nasty cases, dismay. The staff generally thought that the report was the Head's business, and it must be admitted that, after it all, life went on much the same as before.

At that time I had my final run of class teaching. It was rewarding and enjoyable. The leavers' class of 14/15 years old had not yet been too heavily creamed off by eleven plus transfer to grammar schools and there was a fair range of ability. I wanted to bring life into the classroom, and to this end, timetable space was found for what were then called 'local studies' - the City of Liverpool, with special reference to the immediate neighbourhood. The movement of shipping was reported in the local Press, and the boys adopted a ship and pinpointed its movement with flags on the world map. The small 'tramp' steamers, which carried their cargoes on an ad hoc basis from port to port around the world were the most instructive. A class fund, to which they seemed to contribute without demur, provided four daily newspapers from the heavy to the tabloid. The front pages displayed for their judgement differing views as to what event during the past twenty-four hours was considered the most worthy of attention.

Towards the end of the summer term, when their schooldays were drawing to a close, I gave a talk on sex. It was factual, without moral content. I had learnt that secondary schoolchildren are more impressed by what you do than what you say. Questions were invited and some were asked. Afterwards I felt that, except in the medical sphere, they had little to learn. It was the one lesson in the school year when you could have heard a pin drop.

I was fortunate to be supported by the enthusiasm of young staff ready to work as a team outside the classroom. The annual Christmas concert, when each class had to contribute an item, fostered a sense of common purpose. Most of the staff attended the summer camp. Our friendship extended beyond the school building. Some of us were acquiring our first cars, then a status symbol. In the immediate post-war years, due to scarcity, new cars were rationed to essential users. The buyer had to covenant not to sell his car before a specified time had elapsed. Supply and demand ensured that used cars cost more than the new model. In our Austin 7's and Ford Anglias we held what we were pleased to call rallies into North Wales, accompanied by our families. The resulting sense of community and shared enterprise was helped, perhaps made possible, by the size of the school. Before the phrase had currency, small was beautiful.

After four years the bottom fell out of this congenial world. The Emergency Teacher Training Colleges had completed their work, and the appointed Deputy Head, whose place I had been taking, returned to duty. I went back to the ranks and less attractive surroundings. Wellington Road, not far from the docks, was back to redbrick and the turn of the century.

The Headmaster, Harry Parker, had an effervescent personality. In his company the world seemed to take on a rosier hue. Perhaps there was a religious background. The customary working men's hobbies of that time were greyhounds and pigeons, neither requiring much space at home. It was discovered in school that Smith had raided the pigeon loft of Jones and taken some birds, called mickeys in Scouse dialect. The school was assembled while Harry gave a stern address on a text from the Book of Proverbs: 'Woe to them that lurk privily for the innocent'.

It was not long before Florence Melly's Deputy Head was appointed to a Headship, and I returned to complete a six year stint. It had given a grounding in teamwork between professional adults. I had learned to identify paths of development and to enlist staff support by encouragement and appreciation rather than criticism and the pressure of authority. Pleasant as it was, the year's work programme had become repetitive. It was time to move on, and I applied for Headships.

The third vacancy after two unsuccessful applications was at the school of my recent exile - Wellington Road. Appointment interviews were now becoming less of a trial. At the round table would be seated the Chairman and other members of the Appointments Sub-Committee (political), the Director of Education, or other professional officer according to the importance of the appointment, a representative of the Advisory Staff (the local Inspectors), the Chairman of the school's Governors, and a secretary.

On entering the room, one controlled a mad impulse for flight, or a suicidal attempt at humour by asking if the vacant chair was reserved. The Chairman of the Governors was the Vicar of the Anglican Church in whose parish the school was situated. He asked me my views on the teaching of religion. I replied that I would rather not have it taught at all than taught perfunctorily. I was surprised to be appointed.

Wellington Road is off Park Road, which is part of the old No. 1 tram route leading south-east from the city centre to the Dingle, Aigburth and Garston. Named after the Duke, whose statue is aloft on a pillar near St George's Hall, it leads straight down to the docks. Those who named the streets, about the middle of the nineteenth century, had a swift change of interest from state to church and named succeeding streets after Moses, Isaac, Jacob and David. It was called the Holy Land.

The school building, probably built soon after the start of compulsory education, was shared by the Boys' and Girls' Departments. The girls had the ground floor and outside playground, the boys the first floor and playground on the roof. Each shared the assembly hall/gymnasium in the basement. They were independent, self-contained departments, with a Head Master and a Head Mistress who could work together, or not, as they decided. I was fortunate to have a congenial working partner over a four-year stint.

Wellington Road School

From the bay window of the Head Master's room stretched a view over the Mersey, past the copper-domed tower of the Birkenhead Town Hall and on a clear day across the Wirral to North Wales, the Clwyd Range, and its highest point Moel Famau. The woodwork rooms were on the other side of the main road at Upper Park Street Primary School. Dinners were taken down the road in Mill Street, at the Florence Institute, founded in 1889 by Mr. Bernard Hall in memory of his daughter Florence, 'to serve as a club for the poor boys of the neighbourhood'. Among the Liverpool boys'clubs it enjoyed the prestige of seniority.

During the intervening holiday thoughts turned to the coming change of status. I had lived beneath Head Masters from the age of five, a presiding authority which appeared and re-appeared, in the flesh, and in the mind, not to be ignored. Now I was up there where the buck stopped. The prospect was welcome. I had served the apprenticeship, and thought I knew how a school ticked. I would build on the foundations already laid by the work of colleagues over the years. A priority was to maintain a climate in which staff would feel content to work.

An immediate necessity was to appoint a new part-time Secretary, the previous one having decided to retire at the same time as her Head Master. The Education Office sent along a lady from their waiting list. I was conscious of my inexperience in making this appointment, and enlisted the services of the retiring Secretary to sit in with me at the interview. She indicated her full approval of the candidate, who gave excellent service to the school over a period of years.

Immediately after my appointment Sam Tiller had told me that the school 'was in good heart'. Mr. S.W. Tiller, M.A. was Liverpool's Chief Inspector of Schools. Appointed in 1939 to a service disintegrating by evacuation at the outbreak of war, he was to guide the progress of the primary and secondary schools for twenty six years. I had met him for the first time on returning from war service, and was to see him for the last time in 1990, when he helped with background information in the preparation of this book.

The staff offered a wide age range, from the experienced to the beginner, with Heads of Departments, though not then described as such, well-versed in their specialities. An engaging colleague was the caretaker Sam Hind. An active member of the local mission church, with white hair, twinkling eyes and fresh complexion, his integrity and friendliness were no doubt part of his religion. At our first meeting he advised me gently not to lock my cupboards. An intruder would force them anyway. Before he retired he told me his boyhood story, which he then regarded, needlessly, as a rather discreditable escapade. It seems that on leaving school to become a clerk in a city office, he chose to walk to work along the dock road, beneath the bowsprits of the sea-going sailing vessels moored in line, bow first. He fell in love with a four-masted barque, the 'Arabella'. On his way home he went aboard to offer his services to the skipper. 'Don't be a fool' he was told. 'Stick to your desk'. He decided to become a stowaway, got up during the night to avoid his parents, collected a loaf from the kitchen, and with only the yellow gas lamps for company, made his way along the dock road to the ship, slipped aboard and hid in a locker. Some of the crew found him and looked after him until the ship sailed. Two days out into the Irish Sea they took him to the skipper who was standing aloft on the forecastle. The skipper looked at him without a word, then hit him so hard that he knocked him into the gunwale. So to the galley, where he worked for the one hundred and thirteen days it took to reach Port Adelaide in Australia. The hardships afloat and the rough seas ended his romance. He jumped ship and in due course worked his passage home.

There were, however, as in all concerns, some less capable than others. At that time there was no dismissal of teachers for inefficiency or inadequacy. Only criminal involvement or a moral lapse meant departure from the profession. It was, therefore, with some apprehension that I sat in on the lesson of a young teacher who was reported to be in difficulties. Surprisingly, perhaps owing to my presence, there was no disorder in the room, but he appeared to be giving his lesson to one or two boys on the front row, while the others chatted together. He was clearly unable to hold the attention of a group. During our subsequent conversation he agreed that he was at a loss in the classroom. He had come into teaching, he said, to have the advantage of further education. I pointed out that as time went on his lessons day after day would be of no use to classes, and a continuing frustration and embarrassment to himself. It was a relief to all when shortly afterwards he left teaching for a business appointment.

Wellington Road, like other inner city schools, was a school for the poor, housed in the long terraces surviving from Victorian times. The reports of the Attendance Officers, later called Welfare Officers, on their weekly visits to school to collect attendance records, testified to the harsh, unpleasant living conditions. There was juvenile petty crime, though not on the scale of later years. The Police Authority, where it was required, had appointed serving policemen as Juvenile Liaison Officers, to visit, in plain clothes, school and home, and to advise, and if possible rehabilitate young offenders. Our Sergeant Turner's reports on home conditions enabled the school to handle the boys with greater understanding.

The ever-present and demanding care of the underprivileged brought together in a fraternal relationship the professionals - altruistic, stoical, or exasperated - who commuted daily to work among them - the clergy, the school teachers, the doctors and nurses, the school meals organisers, the attendance officers, and the representatives of voluntary bodies. We met regularly at our luncheon club, inviting speakers who could contribute to our discussions. Not far away in Nile Street, was the University Settlement, founded in 1906 to give students the means of studying at first hand the problems of the socially deprived. The Warden, John Mays, held what would now be called workshops, for representatives of the schools and the welfare agencies. Later he was to publish a standard work on the life of the young in the inner city of Liverpool - 'Growing up in the City', and to move to the Eleanor Rathbone Chair of Sociology in the University. These regular meetings and the exchange of ideas and experience, gave us an understanding of what could, and could not, reasonably be expected of boys who spent only a proportion of their time in the orderly and disciplined routine of school.

As time passed and the necessary and welcome contacts with parents became part of the job, I realised that in the education of our charges we were, whether we liked it or not, in partnership with their parents. Whether the partnership was effective or not depended on the home response and, in the first instance, on the initiative of the school. The idea of Parent-Teacher Associations was becoming a regular topic in the education press. To some in the profession it was suspect, as bringing a risk of uninformed interference in school affairs. The proposal was more interesting to Heads than to teachers, less aware from a classroom base of the homes behind the scholars, and naturally reluctant to come back in the evening after a day's work in the classroom.

Enquiries brought to school a father and mother willing to help. This was the starting point for evening meetings at school addressed by a speaker. I recall Mrs. Molly Cumella, well-known for her outspoken radical views, and Mrs. Ethel Wormald, education spokesperson for the Liverpool Labour Party. I learned much from their talks to the few mothers who attended. They knew the working women of Liverpool and could talk to them like a parent. As I sat through the meetings, nominally the Chairman, I learned also that these experienced ladies did not rate my observations highly. I am sure their judgement was correct.

Morning assembly was part of the Head's duties, taken in turn with the Girls' Department, a short non-denominational service, routine announcements, and the occasion for setting standards. On first contemplating a Headship I had to face the anomaly, or was it the immorality, of an agnostic taking the prescribed religious service at morning assembly. The association of Church and School has a long history. The churches from the eighteenth century had played a prominent part in the provision of public education in the schools and teacher training colleges. Their inability to make proper provision for the population as a whole, and the demand by some sections of opinion that public education should be independent of the churches, led to the intervention of the state and the 1870 Education Act, which made it possible for all children in the country to have a school place. From that time Church Schools and State Schools have co-existed in partnership. A succession of Acts of Parliament dealt with this 'dual system'. In return for contributing to the repair and maintenance of the buildings, the Church Schools were authorised, in varying degrees according to the proportion of their contribution, to make their own arrangements in regard to the appointment of governors and teaching staff and, most importantly, in religious instruction.

The arguments for and against compulsory religious education began with the approach of a State Education system in the latter half of the last century. On the one hand the Churches and some parents maintained the right of parents to have their children brought up in the religion of their choice. They stressed the moral content of religious belief and contended that such instruction in childhood lays the foundation of good character. Opposing views are advanced with equal conviction by the humanists, who can trace their dissent back to the last century, and fearless protagonists such as Charles Bradlaugh and, in this century, H.G. Wells and Bertrand Russell. They questioned the desirability and indeed the morality of imprinting religious dogma on children before their critical faculty has developed, during their impressionable years when they are captive audiences in the classroom and the assembly hall. They are not short of modern instances of the consequences, in Northern Ireland and abroad. The proper place for religious instruction, they say, is in the Church and the home.

In successive Education Acts politicians, sensitive to the pressure of the Anglican and Roman Catholic Churches in both Houses of Parliament, and aware of the indifference of the majority of parents, followed the line of least resistance. Church schools retained the right to teach the doctrines of their Church. Religious instruction and daily worship in State schools was made compulsory based on syllabuses agreed by the parties concerned - the Churches, the teachers and the Education Authorities.

The earnest and forceful arguments of the Church lobby in favour of compulsory religious instruction, and subsequent legislation, showed either ignorance or unconcern at what would happen, and did happen, in the maintained (State) schools at the end of the processes they had initiated. As a probationer teacher attending my first summer camp I could only be a listener to experienced colleagues when tongues were loosened in the staff marquee. The talk turned to R.E., then called Scripture. The respected Headmaster of a large school listened to his juniors and then gave his verdict: "The buggers know that ninety per cent of (men) teachers are agnostics, but they'd rather have it taught by them than not at all".

Experience has confirmed this robustly expressed view. For the majority of teachers called upon to take it, R.E. was an unwelcome duty, and scholars of secondary age were aware of it. The spread of scientific knowledge through the press and media did not reinforce the supernatural element in religious belief. And their morality was formed by the outlook and attitudes of the home, in turn dependent upon the home's reaction to the good fortune, or lack of it, which they found to be their lot in contemporary society. There is little doubt that enforced religious instruction did more harm than good to the causes espoused by its protagonists.

The legislation contained conscience clauses. Parents could withdraw their children from the subject and the assembly. Teachers could decline the subject and would not be penalised. These well-intentioned safeguards were rarely used. Parents are reluctant to draw attention to their children among their peers in school. Teachers similarly with a career to build would avoid open dissent. Could a Headship be considered for a candidate unable to take assembly?

The politicians' involvement in religious education is not made easier by the arrival and growth of immigrant religions, who claim for themselves the same public funding allowed to the Anglican and Roman Catholic Churches. If granted, and in equity it cannot be refused, it will lead to separation from the host community and perhaps to a proliferation of the religious conflict found in some parts of Asia. On the reverse side of the coin, it may induce Parliament seriously to consider legislation leading to the end of subsidies for denominational schools.

Thus I found myself, no doubt like many of my colleagues, the innocent and unwilling legatee of the unyielding determination of the Church establishment, the concessions of Government and the apathy of the general public. I was in a job that I liked, which provided the opportunity of service to those who were not my paymasters. The latter were happily at a distance. My daily employers were my children. They might stretch me, and at times exasperate me, but they were congenial partners in the enterprise of teaching. All this I could retain as a class teacher, but I had tasted the satisfaction of organisation and leadership and the prospect of forty years of class teaching was a daunting one. Like the governments who had landed teachers in this dilemma I compromised, with the proviso that I would reduce to a minimum the elements of which my conscience was afraid.

I was now to make my first close acquaintance with school governors. The last school had survived happily without them. Their functions and identities were at that time unknown to the general public and indeed to parents and serving teachers. By a subtle but unjustifiable act of discrimination the ladies and gentlemen who performed the same service for primary schools, were described as managers. Obliged to meet at least once a term, they also met, as required, for staff appointments. Their role then was less active than it later became, - to comment, express an opinion, and to vote, if necessary, on an appointment. And in fact as lay people visiting school infrequently, they were not qualified to do more. Our Chairman was the Vicar of the nearby Anglican church, to be followed, on his departure to an Essex parish, by Mr. Austin Rawlinson. In his appointment I had a personal interest. Austin Rawlinson, enjoying the reputation of a former Olympic swimmer, had now retired from the Liverpool police force, and had taken an interest in schoolboy swimming. He came to one of our swimming lessons at Steble Street baths and, noting his obvious concern for the boys, I suggested to him that he might consider a closer association with the schools and become a governor. This he did, and brought to our proceedings a welcome contribution of non-professional common sense. His work for the encouragement of swimming in Liverpool was recognised when a new swimming bath at Speke was named after him.

Some of the special events which must punctuate and hopefully illuminate school routine were already in place - the annual swimming gala, the old boys' reunion, the prize-giving, now made the occasion of a display of work. In December there were rehearsals for the carol service, held in the Anglican Cathedral. There we were under the guidance of Canon Jacobs, who described his position in the church hierarchy as 'not a big gun, only a pop-gun'. As the boys sang and spoke their readings in one of the largest cathedrals in the world, we were aware of the humanity which extended a welcome regardless of status.

We also enjoyed and profited by a friendly interest from another quarter. The Ship Adoption Society had been formed to link school and ship.

They would become acquainted with each other by exchange of correspondence. The school would learn something of the requirements of a sea-going career and, before the era of easy foreign travel, of a seaman's impression of far-away places. Our ship was the T.S.M.V. (Twin Screw Motor Vessel) Clan Macdonald. The Clan Line was one of the shipping lines founded in the second half of the last century to take advantage of the growing foreign trade made possible by the steam ship. Captain Hogg took more than a passing interest in us. He, and occasionally his wife when she accompanied him, would send us an account of their voyage. Sometimes a cadet would present a crewman's view, with information of officers' duties, or the ship's gear.

On my last visit Captain Hogg had been promoted to the command of the S.S. Argyllshire, the line's newest ship. He entertained us in his cabin, as lavishly appointed as a hotel suite, where Mrs. Hogg held court with the ease of an accomplished hostess.

As each summer a Fourth Year left and a First Year was admitted, it became clear that we were not a preferred school. Dingle Vale, half a mile down the road, had been purpose built in 1938 to meet Hadow requirements, with the premises and equipment now taken for granted as the minimum provision for secondary education. Parents, it was said, thought it was a sort of college. Ambitious parents naturally sought admission for their children, who, with home support, were likely to perform better in school and to respond more willingly to school requirements. As time passed teachers were attracted to a more responsive school environment and the calibre of staff would reflect the difference. It was a see-saw effect apparent in cities and towns big enough to have schools within easy reach of each other. The market town, with only one secondary school, was not open to this discrimination. It was a fact of life in a city education set-up, where the Authority had not the means to raise building standards in all schools simultaneously.

At the end of their school life, then at the age of fifteen, it was customary for the boys to leave the building on the last day without official recognition that this was a turning point in their lives. Some might say goodbye to an admired teacher, but nothing more. To mark this occasion a leavers' service was introduced, with an appropriate ceremony, an address from myself, and the presentation of testimonials. These were a statement of the boy's achievements and character as observed by his schoolmasters, to be used in seeking employment. They were not used in grammar schools, where results in public examinations were considered to be enough.

I found it a moving occasion, and indeed, as time passed, the boys, without prompting from school, would appear in their best suits. What should I tell them? That employment, while it would provide the satisfaction and recognition of a wage, would be a shock to their sense of seniority acquired at the top end of the school. Since the age of five they had been in an institution of which they were the sole purpose. In commerce or industry they would be back again as beginners and should not expect the consideration they had had from their teachers. But with honesty, reliability, punctuality, readiness to work, and a spirit of-enterprise, they would lay the foundation of a successful career. Finally they were told that they themselves had composed their testimonials. The School had written the record they had made. The atmosphere of a threshold being passed to an uncertain immediate future made the event a memorable finale to their school career.

Testimonial writing was not a risk-free exercise. In each year there were one or two boys who, through inability or persistent absence, had made no impression, and little was known of them. Their testimonials recorded only their presence on the school roll. The father of one such boy came to see me, testimonial in hand. This, he said, was no use at all. How could his son get a job with it? His tone suggested that I must do better. I pointed out that I could only record his son's performance. He thought that was irrelevant.

It was unusual for a boy to ask to see me with a career enquiry unaccompanied by his parents. I recall one such occasion when a good-looking, fair-haired boy came to my room to enquire how he could qualify as a draughtsman. His education had been interrupted by a heart condition and his classroom performance was below average. I was sorry I could give him no encouragement. His name was Ronald Wycherley. Later he became the pop-star Billy Fury, destined, in some respects, to leave his schoolmasters behind.

The years went by quickly. The school appeared to be performing as well as it could in view of its clear limitations. The staff were co-operative and responsive to suggestions. I took to the Art Master, a passage from Richard Carrington's 'A Guide to Earth History':- 'If we imagine that the whole of the earth's history were compressed into a single year, then on this scale the first eight months would be completely without life. The following two months would be devoted to the most primitive creatures, ranging from viruses and single-celled bacteria to jelly fish, while the mammals would not appear until the second week in December. Man, as we know him, would have strutted on the stage at about 11.45 p.m. on 31st December, and the age of written history would have occupied little more than the last sixty seconds on the clock.' After a while, along the corridor, appeared a series of pictures illustrating this astonishing sequence.

Vacancies for Head Teachers, secondary (except for grammar schools) and primary, were advertised only in the Bulletin circularised to all Liverpool schools from the Education Office. It was felt that in a large city there was enough ability and experience to provide suitably qualified candidates. The practice also fostered a sense of loyalty to the Authority. Towards the end of my fourth year at

Wellington Road the appointment of Head Master of Gilmour Secondary Boys' School was advertised. Gilmour, in the Allerton district, was a suburban school with a strong sporting reputation, spoken of as a 'good' secondary modern. I was content to wait a while but this seemed an opportunity, which was not likely to occur often, to put experience to work in a wider context. After the now familiar routine of application and interview over the round table I was appointed.

Four years perhaps had been too short a time to present an education philosophy and hopefully put it into practice. I had wanted to repeat at Wellington Road the experience of the previous school Florence Melly, and bring the staff together in a social relationship. But I learned that in education too there are horses for courses and what is right for one school may not be right for another. Nevertheless the expressions of goodwill before leaving suggested that the approach was promising.

I had first heard of Gilmour during my probationary year, when the Head had referred to it with some envy as a school 'with its own assembly hall'. It had been opened in 1929, its name shared by the neighbouring girls' and primary schools. Hamilton Boswell Gilmour, who had died in 1903, made his fortune as a merchant and spent his remaining years in public service, notably in association with several schools and colleges. The Boys' School was officially referred to as Gilmour Heath Road. But the local authority schools of that time were generally described by the name of their road or street, and Gilmour Boys' was generally spoken of as Heath Road.

The first Head Master, A.J. Mason, came from the nearby Duncombe Road School. Records note that, numbers of his new school being less, his salary on transfer was reduced from £510 to £474 per annum. The first entry in the Log Book states that the school was opened on Wednesday morning August 14th 1929 with 287 boys on roll. In following pages the repercussions of great events sounded an echo:

Friday 1 September 1939 ... evacuation of schoolchildren was ordered to commence

8 - 19 September ... Head Master and Staff engaged in Air Raid Precautions Survey

8 September 1941 ... Confidential. The Board of Education in a recent Administrative Memorandum have suggested that, in order to avoid any uncertainty arising in the schools as to their position in the event of invasion by the enemy, Head Teachers should be informed in confidence that, in the event of such invasion, the schools should remain open unless and until authoritative instructions are received by them to the contrary and that such instructions may, in certain circumstances, be issued by the Regional Commissioner, and not through the Local Education Authority.

Peace VE (Victory in Europe) Day. On the evening of Monday 7 May 1945 it was announced that the

Gilmour Boys' School.

following day would mark the end of hostilities in Europe and that that day and the following day would be national holidays.

The building, an object of envy in the 1930's, was now inadequate by the standards of 1958 - eight classrooms along a main ground floor corridor and six larger rooms for specialist subjects, an assembly hall/gymnasium and small ancillary rooms. The adjacent playing fields, of some two and a half acres, had provided the training ground for the school's athletic prowess.

The Staff offered a welcome range of qualification and experience. The retiring Head, R.S. Simpson, appointed in November 1936, was ending twenty two years' service to the school. During this time he had become a polio victim and had not been able to leave his room during the last seven years. It seemed sensible, during my first year, to confer with him and profit by his experience. On two or three occasions I went after school to his house in the Wavertree Garden Suburb and, over afternoon tea with his wife and himself, felt as though playing the part of a runner in a relay race, taking the baton from my predecessor to hand it on in turn on retirement. I was unaware that events would overtake and overturn my confident forecast.

Considering the Head's disability it is a tribute to his personality and the professional competence of the staff that the discipline of the school had not been eroded. But there were problems, not of the school's making. Soon after my arrival the caretaker had commiserated with me. He was sorry, he said, that I had not been at the school 'when it was nice'. He was referring to the recent influx of boys from 'Garston under the bridge', an enclave of terrace houses on the banks of the Mersey, approached under the railway which served the Garston docks. I came to admire the outspoken independence of this closely knit community. They had had their own school, Banks Road, taking their children from the age of five to fifteen. Reorganisation had changed it into a primary school, sending the seniors to Gilmour, a mile away. The ensuing difficult mix of contrasting social backgrounds was to add to the acceptable problems of discipline in a boys' secondary school.

The idea of discipline as a requirement for efficient teaching seems to be out of fashion. In education, as elsewhere, the pendulum of sentiment swings, during the 1960's from a strict regime which came to be thought too restrictive for the free development of personality, to a more relaxed set-up in the classroom and in the school community. Firm views have been expressed on both sides of the argument. In the view of those in the front line of class teaching discussion starts by accepting the reality that schoolchildren in classes will not work without some form of control. They prefer to lark about and be amused and in a class of thirty there will be jokers to provide the required entertainment. What should be the nature of this control?

Age difference requires a different approach for primary and secondary children and experience qualifies me to speak only of secondary schools. If courses are planned carefully for the age group, if lessons are as interesting as possible using modern aids to learning, if the teacher is competent and the school well organised, surely disciplinary measures are not needed? Alas, this was not the case. A typical class of thirty would have been likely to have two or three natural students, ready to work without supervision. The majority would work if necessary. But there would be two or three, perhaps from disturbed homes, perhaps from homes which made a point of challenging authority, perhaps by nature of unstable personality who, unchecked, would do what they could to interrupt lessons and draw attention to themselves. Most of them would have already been noticed for repeated absence, lateness, failure to bring equipment for lessons, leaving the building without permission. The harmful effects of these on class and school was out of all proportion to their numbers. The energy of the class teacher, already employed in preparing, delivering, and supervising a lesson, was stretched by having to cope with persistent behaviour problems. These, when referred to senior staff, took up time and energy in interviews with the offenders and their parents which might last over a period of weeks.

It was felt in the profession that behaviour problems in school were a side-effect of the permissive society which became accepted in the 1960's. How could teachers, in their view, with credibility insist on standards against a background of laxity in an increasing number of homes. They wryly reflected that society appeared to wish them to do so, while at the same time failing to provide, through the homes and the authorities, the support by way of effective sanctions that the school required.

The relaxation of rules hitherto considered necessary for good schooling was hastened by the Children and Young Persons Act of 1969, which reflected the current sentiment that children who break the law should be dealt with by a therapeutic approach rather than by punitive measures. Teachers thought that this move of itself contributed to a greater degree of lawlessness and undisciplined behaviour among young people. The Act instituted a long procedure of legal action for delinquent schoolchildren. This seemed, by its nature, to be counter-productive. If an offence was committed, either outside or in the school situation, an immediate response was called for. Delay seemed to condone the offence in the mind of the child concerned and in the eyes of his schoolmates. The emphasis of the Act was on consultation at all levels and it was doubtful if a young offender realised the nature and severity of his offence if he or she was brought before the court weeks, or months, after committing it. A backlog of cases might lengthen delay, and give the impression in the minds of fellow-pupils that offences could be committed with impunity. But teachers generally were slow to protest openly, thinking it might reflect on their professional competence, and thus failed to attract the concern of the authorities and the public which a deteriorating situation demanded.

What then was the remedy for misbehaviour which interfered with the education of most schoolchildren? Common sense suggested removal from the school. Should a Head be empowered to exclude from school? There would be no shortage of those who, relieved of the legal obligation to attend school, would by misbehaviour take the opportunity to leave school and form gangs to roam the neighbourhood. The Local Education Authority did what could be done, and spent substantial amounts to ease the problem, short of actively supporting teachers in dealing with the miscreants. Special classes for slow learners in certain schools, education guidance units for cases of school phobia, a psychological service, remedial teaching teams, and so on, measures reflecting the spirit of the Children and Young Persons Act. Their impact on the incidence of classroom disturbance was not apparent.

Non-selective schools (in schools where there is an element of selection, either by fees or entrance examination, episodes of disruption are relatively scarce), and these are the great majority, require an effective and immediate deterrent to disruptive pupils. In the absence of corporal punishment, it means early removal to a less attractive environment, where basic subjects are taught, attendance and punctuality and the bringing to class of simple equipment - pen, pencil, notebook, and good behaviour - are strictly enforced. And here is the crux. Is an Education Authority, with the backing of parents and society, prepared to enforce such corrective measures? If not, disruption will continue, with its lamentable effects on pupils and teachers.

It soon became clear that with a well-qualified staff the standard of subject teaching was high at Gilmour. The Science Master was John Hamilton, later to become Labour leader of the Liverpool City Council, and to be caught up in the turmoil which accompanied the advent of the Militant Tendency. I look back with respect and affection on the Deputy Head Jim Norris. We were of similar age and had been together on the staff of Anfield Road School at the beginning of the war. He was called up for the Headship of Gilmour, a courtesy extended by the Authority to Deputies when the Headship of their school became vacant. As some half dozen of us waited in the ante-room, he addressed us

'Whichever of you gentlemen is appointed - my full support.' Of north country farming stock, he was deliberate in speech and manner. The first of the teaching staff to arrive at school in the morning, he would, from time to time, express his philosophy in a few well-considered maxims - 'It's good every day to do something you don't want to. It's better to do something you don't want to for somebody you don't like.' 'It does a man no harm occasionally to eat humble pie.' (I wondered if this was directed at me.) His sense of humour revealed a countryman's shrewdness. The bell for change of lessons was then rung manually from the office. When asked how many times the bell should be rung on each occasion he replied - 'Ring three times for the beginning and change of lessons. At going home time the merest ping will suffice.'

Jim was to die prematurely just before retirement. As a tribute to him these are his thoughts on the teaching of slow learners in a secondary boys' school, put together at my request -

> 'The first essential for such a class is a room of their own, where art and light craft materials can be available, and where work may be left out and continued when opportune, since much of their work will be of a practical nature.
>
> In such a room centres of interest and simple projects can be developed, and a library formed for reading and reference, with catalogues,

descriptive leaflets and similar. Machine parts of cars, motor-bikes, cycles, radios, are useful references for oral and written work.

Individual attention is essential to success and the starting point is the boy's own interests. Boys respond differently to work programmes, some requiring a practical, some an academic approach. A vocational bias is a stimulus to routine work. Some boys have a desire to help and will take pleasure in doing the odd jobs round the classroom. Some work well from written instructions, others from oral guidance.

They learn well in Woodwork, Metalwork and Physical Education. But avoid too much specialisation and the consequent moving about from one room to another. Regular changes of work under guidance are helpful, as also a mixture of individual and group activity. All the lads desire to please and much anti-social behaviour is a defence put up to give them time to think in an emergency.

All the above depends on the right kind of teacher being available, in particular one who does not consider misbehaviour as a personal affront to himself.'

It was Jim who suggested that we should introduce a Fifth Form for boys who wished to stay on and take an external examination. External examinations, set by University Examination

Boards grouped in regions, had been the reserve of the grammar schools. The old School Certificate, first introduced in 1917, had been superseded in 1951 by the General Certificate of Education Ordinary Level and Advanced Level. These, especially Advanced Level, were geared to University requirements, and were beyond the abilities of the majority of secondary school pupils. It was ironic that during the years following the formation of the secondary modern schools after the war, the freedom of these schools from external examination pressures was regarded as an asset, providing an opportunity for experiment in devising courses for the wide range of abilities and background. But as novelty faded and experiments were either integrated into courses or found unsuitable, interest began to turn to examining bodies which provided tests of a less demanding nature - the College of Preceptors, the Royal Society of Arts, and the Union of Lancashire and Cheshire Institutes. It was now felt that for the interested minority a suitable examination would provide an incentive for steady work and a leaving qualification, and that the school would benefit by having a responsible group of seniors to set standards and exercise the duties of a prefect body.

Much has been written on the use and misuse of examinations. When directed to a specific purpose - a professional, craft, or other qualification, they need no defence and may, indeed, be necessary in the public interest. When used in schools where pupils were captive candidates at an impressionable age, care was needed. Internal routine examinations provided a stimulus for most pupils and an assessment of progress for the teacher. But there was an important proviso - that they should be so constructed and administered as not to develop a sense of failure in pupils who were doing their best to master school subjects.

It was generally admitted in the profession that public examinations could become a strait-jacket into which school courses were fitted. As early as 1943 the Norwood Report, set up 'to consider suggested changes in the secondary school curriculum and the question of School Examinations in relation thereto', had put forward the principle that examinations should follow the curriculum and not determine it. Yet it was difficult enough for parents, attempting to judge the quality of a school from the outside, not to accept examination results as a convenient yardstick. But did the school with the best results devote too much time to exam subjects at the expense of others necessary for a balanced education? Did it overload its pupils with too much homework?

An even stronger influence on the pursuit of external examination results was their use by employers in selecting applicants for appointments, a practice of which parents were fully aware. Whether performance in 'O' levels was an accurate predictor of performance in employment has not apparently been researched. But the influence of career prospects and the associated parental concern on the secondary curriculum was not in doubt. In the interests of an all-round education free from undue pressure it would have been better, in the view of teachers, if employers had administered their own examinations for prospective employees, constructed to meet their special requirements. In the belief, therefore, that examinations are a good servant but a bad master and, in consultation with interested parents, a Fifth Form was established, and for the rest of the school's life played its part as planned.

The co-operation of interested parents in these projects was not a problem. The current idea of Parent-Teacher Associations was discarded and a Parents' Association was formed. Their committee met regularly under my chairmanship. The Head was clearly the most effective link between the school and themselves. Their services, now commonplace, were an innovation at the time. Fund-raising events provided us with an organ and annual prizes for each of five year groups 'for boys who have made noteworthy progress by hard work and determination, and who would not otherwise be prizewinners.' Their most valuable function was the regular consultation between them and myself. There was frankness on either side and a resulting mutual confidence.

The Summer Fair at the Gilmour Boys' School. Centre, the Deputy Head, Jim Norris.

It did not take long after my appointment to appreciate the results of the work which had been done by a succession of schoolmasters over the years. The high standard of Gilmour's sporting achievement was evident to parents and friends at the Annual Swimming Gala when the best performers swam with expert proficiency. The passage of school leavers into employment was well provided for by interview with the Local Authority's Juvenile Employment Officer, now supplemented by a Careers Convention, when interested firms and Further Education Colleges were provided with accommodation to display their literature and give advice. Few innovations were needed - an Open Day for parents to look at school work and activities was added to the annual prize-giving, a Summer Fair in the playing field, when stalls and competitions offered a meeting place for staff, parents and friends, and a Carol Service in All Souls Church, Mather Avenue.

It was clear, however, that for the Head the immediate priority would be a continued effort to bring the buildings up to parity with more fortunate secondary schools. In informal meetings with Local Authority officials, Her Majesty's Inspectors, and others who could help, and in public on a succession of Speech Days, I presented the case for modernisation and extension. The Parents' Committee, on their part, made direct representations to the Minister of Education.

It was at Gilmour that the effects of the approaching permissive society were first felt in school. The open bike shed, storing some hundred cycles in 1958, was empty when I left nine years later. Interference and theft had made it unusable. Though I felt in some measure responsible at the time, with hindsight it was a barometer of changing standards. The enforcement of school attendance slackened off, made more difficult by the ease with which medical certificates could be obtained. Children whose absence was supported by a doctor's note would be seen playing in the street. This was so common that a deputation from the Liverpool Head Teachers Association took the case to the Liverpool Branch of the British Medical Association, and later to the Local Medical Council. The doctors' representatives would accept no responsibility for taking school attendance into account when they dispensed certificates. They were concerned, they said, with the doctor/patient relationship. The reports of School Attendance Officers of their experiences when carrying out their duties were a commentary on the times. Efforts to obtain admittance to a house where the residents were at home and watching him through a window, had to be continued in devious ways. Some boys had found for themselves a job in Garston Market, where the Officer would go on patrol to catch them. He no doubt received special commendation for discovering that the proprietor of a furnishing stall concealed his juvenile assistant in a roll of linoleum standing upright.

Illegal entries into the building were becoming more frequent. Arriving at school one Monday morning, my room recalled the havoc of war-time bombing. The locked door had been prised open, and the intruder, perhaps after finding nothing of value, had gone on a rampage of destruction, defecated into a prize trophy, and attempted to tear pages out of the Log Book which was then of no further use. It was thought for a time that this was the work of an aggrieved former scholar. It turned out that the culprit was a loner, having no connection with the school.

The Arts, too, seemed to respond to liberalising change. Accustomed to the popular tunes of the big bands, one noticed with surprise on the front page of the Liverpool Echo the names of the new groups - the Mindbenders, The Pacemakers, the Beatles. As a boys' school we were not affected in the same way as the girls' schools by late arrivals in the afternoon when the girls had gone down town in the dinner hour to hear and see the Beatles in The Cavern in Mathew Street. But at Gilmour there was more than a passing interest in the group. Paul McCartney's home was in nearby Forthlin Road and John Lennon was a scholar at Quarry Bank, a mile away. Most permissive of all, there was the contraceptive pill.

It was now possible to take part in activities which, though they were outside school, were valuable in school especially to those involved in management. As a teacher representative I began an association with the Teachers' Advisory Committees, which lasted until retirement. The T.A.C.'s, set up after the war, were composed of a majority of serving teachers, with a representative of the Education Authority, and with power to co-opt lay specialists in the subject being investigated. Meeting at the Education Office over as long a period as was required, we prepared reports on subjects referred to us or suggested by ourselves. There was no dearth of these. - The Use of Audio-Visual Media, Performance in the Secondary Schools, The Suspended Child, Sex Education, among many others. After thorough and wide-ranging enquiry and discussion lasting a year or more, a Report was issued. Copies were sent to city councillors, members of the Education Committee, schools, and interested individuals. The Director of Education's Report of 1951/52 observed - 'The value of the Teachers' Advisory Committee lies not only in the opportunity it gives for consultation with the teachers and obtaining their considered opinion on matters of educational policy and practice, but it is a further link in establishing confidence between the teaching staffs on the one hand and the administration on the other.' The teacher members were not so sanguine. They felt that the Authority, for one reason or another, was not in a hurry to implement their recommendations. Nevertheless, the Reports have a relevance and value beyond the concerns of the time, providing guide-lines, if they are followed, based on experience in the schools, for those in Education Authorities on whose decisions the progress and welfare of the schools depend.

Acting as a teacher representative one gradually became aware of the administrative set-up centred in the Education Office in Sir Thomas Street. Built in 1898 it was still occupied in 1991, having absorbed its immediate neighbours to meet the needs of an expanding service. Here local politicians and civil servants co-existed, tolerating, on the one hand, what the professionals regarded as the Utopian aspirations of the politicians and, on their side, the intransigence of the professionals in not carrying them out forthwith. The professionals had the advantage of security of tenure. The politicians faced possible dismissal at the next election.

The twin summits were occupied by the Chairman of the Education Committee and the Director of Education, the former nominated by the party in office at the time. The Director of Education, in some places called the Chief Education Officer, would be a career civil servant working for a Local Authority, perhaps in a small town, perhaps in a city, with overall responsibility for putting into operation party policy over a wide range of educational establishments, from infants' schools to colleges of further education, and their many ancillary services.

The history of education in Liverpool during the two decades after the war reflected the character and personality of the Director of Education, Harold S. Magnay. Having served an apprenticeship as Director of Education for the South Yorkshire town of Barnsley, he came to Liverpool at the end of the war. I first remember him speaking at the North of England Education Conference in the Winter Gardens at Blackpool, when we sat in our overcoats in an unheated hall in January, 1946. War-time rationing had reserved fuel for more important operations. During the eighteen years of his tenure he provided an account of the problems and achievements of the Liverpool education services in a series of Annual Reports, each containing some one hundred and eighty pages or more. The Introduction of his first Report of 1945/46 gives a flavour of his approach to post-war reconstruction and innovation:-

> *'The work of the Education Committee increases in scope, in intensity and in pace as the beginnings of implementing the Education Act of 1944 are undertaken. It is clear that the full implementation of the Act is a matter of twenty-five or more years and that these first steps must be taken with that long vision. Already the Education Committee, with its scheme of sub-committees, has been reconstituted to follow the functions outlined in the Act. The central office administration has been strengthened by two*

additional responsible officers, and the number and variety of Advisers has been increased by five to meet the expanding needs of the service. The return of men from their five or six years in the Forces, both to the administration and the teaching staffs, has brought an enlivening influence to the whole service, and it is a source of pleasure and pride that these men have so quickly taken up their work again, and are looking forward to the developments in which they will play so important a part.

As a newcomer to Liverpool your Director of Education is impressed by the resilience of the staffs of the Education Service after the severe and disastrous experiences of wartime, by the way in which the teachers so readily and efficiently undertake the organisation of the sports activities of the boys and girls, by the way in which the difficulties of teaching are faced in the appalling conditions of the worst schools, and by the readiness of staffs to take full part in developments which will mean wider and fuller education.

The problems which face us in Liverpool are more complex and difficult of solution than in any other area outside London, but that in itself makes the prospect more exciting. The Ministry of Education recognise this in granting a deferment of the Development Plan for one year in the first instance. It will take more than one or two years to produce a Development Plan with any reality or meaning, and the fundamental factors of movement of population, the proportion of children requiring denominational education in the redeveloped areas, and indeed, the situation and size of those areas themselves require settlement, before the details of an education development plan can be considered.'

THE COMPREHENSIVE DEBATE

The End of the Eleven Plus

As the Gilmour years passed it became clear that we were at the wrong end of 11 plus selection - the examination taken by scholars in their last year at primary school, to select those who would be allowed to proceed to grammar or technical school. During the three decades after the war no single issue preoccupied the partners in education - parents, teachers, administrators - more than the method of transfer from primary to secondary school. Previous misgivings about selection procedures no doubt drew the attention of the Hadow Report as early as 1926 to the problem: 'For the purposes (of transfer) a written examination should be held, and also, where possible, an oral examination. A written psychological test might also be specially employed in dealing with border line cases, or where a discrepancy has been observed between the result of the written examination and the teacher's estimate of proficiency.' From that time secondary selection remained an issue which would not go away. Its opponents hoped it would be made redundant by the introduction of comprehensive secondary education. Its supporters gave time and thought to making it as fair and reliable as possible.

The subject was a continuing and sometimes agonising theme in the Liverpool Director's Reports:-

1947/8

All children in the city between eleven and twelve years of age on 1/8/48 were given an intelligence test in December 1947. These children were also reviewed by the Heads of primary schools, and as a result 4782 candidates were nominated for the Secondary Schools General Entrance Examination. This number includes the candidates who were admitted at the desire of their parents and not on the recommendation of the Heads of schools. On the results 1479 candidates were recommended for admission to High Schools.

1958/9

The Education Committee in September 1958 took decisions to effect important changes in the procedure for admission of pupils to Selective Secondary Schools. The Education Committee had had this most important subject under prolonged and thorough consideration since the autumn of 1955, when they asked the Examinations Board (a local committee) for a report on it. The Board in 1957 made many constructive suggestions. Nevertheless, all the suggestions did not find favour with the

Teachers' Associations. This led the Education Committee to constitute a special sub-committee, consisting of representatives of the Education Committee, the Examinations Board and the Teachers' Associations, which obtained the views of the teachers through their representatives. Many members of the Committee would have preferred a system whereby selection for secondary education was not necessary but all were agreed that, as long as selective secondary schools exist, a method of selection which is impartial and just must obtain, and that everything possible should be done to ensure that the system is as reliable, fair, and humane as it can be made.

It was decided that the Head Teacher of each primary school should be asked to make a quantified assessment of each pupil in the appropriate age group and his/her suitability for education in a selective secondary school. This would count for two fifths of the possible marks, the remaining three fifths being accounted for by tests in English, arithmetic and verbal reasoning. It has always been accepted that the Head Teacher is the person in a position to place pupils in his own school in the proper relative order of merit. The difficulty has been to relate the assessments of the Head Teachers of different schools because of the element of subjectivity in such assessments. To reduce this element of subjectivity, the assessments of the Head Teachers are scaled down against the performance of the children in a test of verbal reasoning given in the primary schools before the main series of tests ..... It was recognised that an age allowance is essential, since otherwise it would be found that the older pupils in the age group scored more marks on the average than the younger pupils.

To accommodate border line cases it was decided that panels of moderators should review all the evidence relating to each child in the border zone, and then make a decision relating to the suitability of each child.

It was agreed that anything in the form of special preparation for the selection tests, and any distortion of the curriculum of the primary school from the form it would take if there were no testing procedure, is undesirable.

1962/3

Junior Leaving Examination *The Education Committee approved a number of recommendations for introduction in the 1963 Junior Leaving Examination ..... The Head Teacher's assessment will be increased from two fifths to half of the final mark. The component for assessing a candidate's suitability for a selective school will be increased.*

Arrangements were made for a computer firm to carry out the many arithmetical calculations and sorting involved in the Junior Leaving Examination. The task of 'programming' was a formidable one, numerous problems having to be solved to ensure that there were no hitches when the time came for the computer to do its work. The success of the operation very much depended on punched cards, and the task of transferring the information on to the cards was undertaken by the City Treasury.

Despite the sustained and exhaustive efforts of the Education Authority, the flaws in the selective procedure remained. On examination day a child might be unwell or handicapped by nervous stress. Parents who could afford it might arrange for private coaching out of school. The proportion of selective places available varied between regions - a child who was unsuccessful in one area might have gained a place in another.

The problem was aggravated by the steadily increasing proportion of the age group who gained selective places. It rose from 19.7% in 1954 to 33.0% in 1964. In that year the proportion in boys' schools, excluding the voluntary church schools, was 40.6%. In the light of the generally accepted view that about 25% of an age group can keep pace with academic courses, the numbers were excessive. The grammar schools were beginning to draw attention to the calibre of their intake. How could these figures be justified against the generally accepted idea that there was a constant and identifiable border line between the clever and the average? There was also a suspicion that the increasing admissions to selective schools were largely due to the pressure of aggrieved parents on their political representatives.

But, in the view of its critics, the over-riding objection to the system as it operated, was the sense of failure it gave to the majority of schoolchildren at a turning point in their career, and the accompanying disappointment and resignation in the home. Gilmour was an example. On the morning after the results came out, the mums would meet while shopping. 'Has he passed?' one would enquire. 'No' was the reply, 'He's got to go to Gilmour.' At the end of the summer term, the parents of boys who would be admitted next September at the beginning of the school year, were invited to an evening meeting, to hear what the school offered and what the school expected of the boys. Of the parents of a hundred and twenty entrants, about fifteen would attend. At a similar meeting in neighbouring Quarry Bank Grammar School there would be a full house. Each year at these meetings I would begin the proceedings by asking them if any of them wanted their sons to go to Gilmour. No parent ever indicated that they did. Their smiles suggested that they didn't want to embarrass me, but that was how it was.

It was clear that in the minds of parents and their children of school age, the secondary modern school was the school you had to go to whether you wanted to or not. Could a proper pride in one's school be built on a sense of failure? Was it right that from the age of eleven 70% of the school population should carry a label of second-best? Would it not be better for a secondary school to admit all the pupils of an area, thus avoiding the invidious distinction? It was these considerations, reinforced by their social priorities, which finally turned the attention of the Labour Party to the option of the comprehensive secondary school.

The idea of a common secondary school entered public debate as early as the 1940's. It was first described as multilateral, a school in which separate streams, graded according to ability, would co-exist in one building. Reformers thought this was too reminiscent of the divisive grammar/technical/ secondary modern set up, and advocated a school structure in which all pupils from an area would attend the same school, in which selection by ability would be reduced to the practicable minimum.

Though the Labour Party in Conference in 1942 supported the principle of a common secondary school, during the six years of the post-war Labour government only a handful of comprehensive schools were opened. Some of them - in Anglesey and the Isle of Man - were established on practical grounds, to meet the needs of a large, sparsely populated admission area. Indeed, apart from a small number of enthusiasts, the initial response of the education establishment was lukewarm. Of the Labour Members of Parliament a number had gone to grammar schools and profited by the selective system. The administration, local and national, were likely to have had an academic education. The teachers too were slow to express support. The secondary moderns saw that they would lose their identity, and the grammar schools feared that their academic standards would be at risk in a larger, unselected school population. But, as time passed, mainly due to the increasing unpopularity of the 11 plus selection procedure, and assisted by the pressure of Labour controlled Local Authorities, by the time of the arrival of a Labour government in 1964, over two hundred comprehensive schools had been opened. Official approval had to wait until Anthony Crosland, the new Minister of Education, enjoined all Local Authorities to submit plans within a year for the comprehensive reorganisation of secondary education, and a year later instructed that future secondary building programmes would only be approved if they were compatible with comprehensive reorganisation.

The progress of comprehensive reorganisation in Liverpool to its partial success in the late 1960's matched the situation in the country as a whole. Its first official appearance was in a Report - "The General Problems of Secondary Education" - made in 1945 by the newly appointed Director of Education Harold Magnay:

> *'The main administration problem is, while securing equality of opportunity for all, to recognise the varying needs of individuals with a practical scheme of school organisation ... The controversy has tended to be focussed upon the relative advantages of organising secondary education in three main types of schools, or else in comprehensive schools ... the real point in dispute is not whether all secondary pupils should have the fullest opportunities to develop their*

abilities and aptitudes through various courses, but whether these courses should all be organised under one roof and one direction, or grouped in various types of schools ... There is not a sufficient body of experience in this country to justify a definitive attitude ... The Director recommends that the secondary schools in this area should be organised in general in three main types of schools, each concentrating on one of the three main types of curriculum, Grammar, Technical and Modern; but when site facilities allow, new schools of different types should be grouped together on the same contiguous site.'

Succeeding Director's Reports marked the advance of a movement politically inspired but not entirely welcome in official circles, where there was some identification with the Grammar Schools. It would also mean an upheaval in the secondary section and a heavy workload.

Report 1954/55

'There has been much criticism of the tripartite (grammar/technical/modern) system, and a number of Local Authorities have already abandoned it in principle and are proceeding with the development, in one form or another, of Common or Comprehensive Secondary Schools, designed to cater for all the senior children in particular areas, regardless of their intellectual or other differences. In this connection unquestionably the most important development in the field of secondary education in the City during this year, has been the resolution of the

> *Education Committee, confirmed in July 1955 by the City Council, (Labour, which had gained control in the municipal elections of that year) that:-*
>
> *Immediate steps be taken to establish comprehensive secondary schools, and that the Director of Education be instructed to prepare a scheme to begin in the year 1956/57.*
>
> *This is a momentous decision, one of the most momentous that has ever been taken by the Education Committee. The full implications cannot yet be foreseen and much detailed work will be required before the precise lines of future development can be plotted out.*

Report 1955/56

> *In November 1955 the Committee received a detailed report from the Director on the possibilities of implementing their resolution that immediate steps should be taken to establish Comprehensive Secondary Schools. In February 1956 a deputation of Committee members and officials visited comprehensive schools in London and, in the same month, a firm proposal for one new comprehensive school was approved for submission to the Ministry of Education.*

This referred to the Gateacre Comprehensive School. Built in 1957 in the south-eastern suburbs, originally as a secondary modern school to accommodate 450 pupils, it was to be enlarged to take 2,040 boys and girls. It took five years to complete the new buildings in three stages, finally opened in 1962 by Kenneth Thompson, Parliamentary Secretary to the Minister of Education. I had attended the opening ceremony of the first instalment of the Building. As the audience gathered in the new assembly hall, impressive in its dimensions and modern design, a stout gentleman, the sole occupant of the platform, who appeared to have escaped the platform party, more than occupied his chair in the centre. He was the chief guest, Sir Edward Boyle, then Parliamentary Secretary to the Minister of Education, known for his liberal views on the left of the Conservative Party. Also on the platform was Eryl Hughes, the school's first Head Master. Previously Head of Science in Anglesey's comprehensive school, he was to pioneer the growth to maturity of Liverpool's earliest and largest comprehensive school until his retirement in the early 1970's.

In 1961 the Labour Party, which had been in office for the last six years, was replaced by a Conservative administration for two years. On returning to office after the municipal elections in 1963, they had clearly decided that progress towards reorganisation had not been good enough.

Report 1962/3

The Education Committee at their meeting in July 1963 resolved:-

'That this Education Committee, believing that comprehensive schools afford the greatest

possible opportunities to boys and girls of all degrees of abilities, affirms that it is its intention that a comprehensive system of secondary education shall be established in Liverpool, and that the County Secondary Schools shall be reorganised accordingly at the earliest possible date, and as a consequence the eleven plus examination shall be abolished, and instructs the Education Sub-Committee, as a matter of urgency, to prepare a scheme directed towards these ends after consultation with the teachers.'

At this point I became involved in the drama of reorganisation. The commitment of the Liverpool Labour Party and the interest of the education press had brought the subject into the staff rooms. The effects on conditions of service were explored and appraised. In secondary modern staff rooms it was observed, not without some relish, that as small schools were amalgamated into larger units, Heads would roll. My Association, the Liverpool Association of Head Teachers, felt that it was time for the teachers to consult together, and organise our response to the coming upheaval. There were four Associations. The National Union of Teachers, formed simultaneously with the introduction of compulsory education in 1870, was nationally the largest and most influential Association, drawing its membership mainly from the primary sector and women teachers. The National Association of Schoolmasters, which began in 1922 as a breakaway from the NUT, represented men teachers in the primary and secondary schools. The Joint Four was an amalgamation of four Associations, of Assistant Masters, Assistant Mistresses, Head Masters and Head Mistresses, serving the interests of the teachers and Heads in the selective schools. The National Association of Head Teachers represented Heads of primary and non-selective secondary schools in the maintained (non fee-paying) sector.

Although the Joint Four at first declined our invitation as premature, the gathering clouds impelled them to action, and a meeting eventually convened with strong delegations from all four Associations. We decided to support comprehensive reorganisation in principle, at the same time expressing our interest and concern in the form it would take. The Joint Four, of course, had no time for the comprehensive idea and would not give up their position at the top of the schools league without a fight. They had the best academic brains on both sides of the teacher's desk, the interest and support of parents, Sixth Forms offering University entrance, and prestige in the community. The difference had been intimated in small ways - separate holiday periods, a holiday on Wednesday afternoons and attendance on Saturday mornings. At Heads' meetings in the Education Office the Grammar School Heads addressed each other by their surnames, the Secondary Modern Heads used their Christian names. However, the Joint Four no doubt decided that they would do better aligned with their colleagues in the other Associations rather than by presenting their case unilaterally.

The many meetings which followed, both amongst ourselves and with the representatives of the Education Authority, lasted over the period of Labour control of the City Council from 1963-1966, and beyond into the Conservative administration of 1967-1971. As Chairman of the Teachers' Panel, I became acquainted with the leading members of the parties concerned. The undisputed leader of the comprehensive lobby was Mrs. Ethel May Wormald. For some years she had been heavily involved, with her husband, in active support of the Liverpool Labour Party. He was a Master at the Liverpool Institute High School, and had been instrumental in launching a highly successful venture - the Mount Street Institute of Further Education. Using the Liverpool Institute building for evening classes, it attracted students who had left school, to follow University Degree and City and Guilds courses.

After the death of her husband Mrs. Wormald devoted a large part of her time and energy to the service of the Labour Party in Liverpool. A graduate and a qualified teacher, though she hadn't, as she said, done any damage in schools, she was the Party's authority and spokesperson on education, and Chairman of the Education Committee from 1955-1961 and from 1963-1966. She found time to hold office in national associations. Her service was recognised by her election as Lord Mayor in 1967-1968 and by her elevation in the Honours List of 1968 as a Dame of the British Empire. Her impact in committee was a measure of her experience and competence, reinforced by her quiet speech and unassuming manner. She was the mainspring of the Labour Party's campaign for comprehensive schools in Liverpool.

Equally capable, though from a different background, was her opposite number, the silver-tongued Mrs Myra Fitzsimmons. With a son at the Liverpool Institute, she was appalled by the thought of a grammar school with a fine tradition becoming a victim of left-wing ideology. She was later to join the Conservative Party and represent them on the City Council for fifteen years, taking leave in 1979 to stand as a Parliamentary candidate for the Kirkdale constituency. In 1989 her public service was recognised by the award of the Order of the British Empire. Throughout the comprehensive negotiations she represented like-minded parents with persistence and skill. She had the character and personality to attract the regard of her opponents.

As meeting followed meeting the lines of battle fell into place. Three Associations were content to prepare and submit a case for a form of reorganisation which would entail the least disturbance in schools. The Joint Four, however, emulated the Roman general who waged war by avoiding battles. They hoped to avert the inevitable by placing long and detailed memoranda before the Authority's representatives at our meetings. Sometimes protagonist met protagonist in single combat. 'So, Councillor', the Grammar School Head would enquire with polished Oxbridge accent, 'you wish to destroy a good school.' The Councillor, well able to cope with the rough and tumble of city politics, was unaccustomed to an antagonist who used the rapier rather than the cudgel. After a pause he would reply, in Liverpool Scouse accent, that he enjoyed a challenge, and this was deemed to settle the matter.

Early discussion centred on the size of the new schools. It was taken for granted that they would have a Sixth Form comparable to those in the existing Grammar Schools. But the disparate numbers of those who stayed on after the statutory leaving age in the Grammar Schools and the Secondary Modern Schools, presented a problem. In the year 1962/1963, when the leaving age was fifteen, the numbers on roll in the different age groups were as follows:-

Age	**Secondary Modern** (81 schools)	**Secondary Technical and Grammar** (33 schools)
14-15	7307 (68%)	3482 (32%)
15-16	1661	3566
Sixth (16-17	331	2111
(17-18	9	855
Form (18-19	1	356

The figures suggested that if, after reorganisation the total number of schools remained the same — 114 — each school would have on average a total of 32 pupils in a three-year Sixth Form, requiring an expensive provision of highly qualified staff to teach GCE Advanced Level and University entrance to a few Sixth Formers. So the acceptable size of a Sixth Form became the basis on which the overall size of the school was to be determined. In the professional jargon, an eight-form entry was to be regarded as a working model. The form-entry was the notional class of thirty pupils when they started secondary school. An eight-form entry would provide a First Year of 240 pupils. Five Year Groups would total 1200 pupils, and this would be increased by the number of Sixth Formers staying on.

The teachers, accustomed to secondary schools of some 400/600, pointed out the drawbacks of schools twice that size. The pupil could not easily identify with a large establishment. The Head would lose personal contact with his charges and would be preoccupied with administrative chores. The school could not enjoy the corporate spirit which inspired a small community.

These objections were aggravated by the recurrent problem of imposing a fresh organisation on buildings designed to meet earlier requirements. Existing buildings were not big enough to accommodate the proposed larger numbers. So, said the Authority, a school must, if necessary, occupy two buildings. This was accepted by the teachers, who suggested that the pupils of the first two or three years would occupy one building under a Head Teacher, proceeding to the second building, also under a Head Teacher, to complete their schooling. There would be a co-ordinated curriculum, the Heads of Departments providing combined syllabuses, where the courses in the junior school would be integrated with the courses in the senior school. The two schools, under one name and identity, would explore the possibilities of exchange of staff, facilities, and combined activities.

We were surprised when this proposal was rejected. The Head Teachers of the two schools, said the Director, C.P.R. Clarke, would not agree. We were not aware that we were a quarrelsome lot. But, if thought advisable, could not the Authority lay down a mandatory procedure, to ensure co-operation between the two schools, and so cover the contingencies which concerned the Director? The Authority, however, were adamant. They stipulated one school and one Head, accommodated in two, possibly three, buildings. The startled teachers pointed out the risks involved in what became known as split premises. It was bad enough settling a class which had moved from one part of a building to another. What would go on when classes moved, unsupervised, along public roads from one building to another? Time would be lost according to the distance. Time-tabling would carry an added complication.

The elected representatives on the Education Committee, conscious that their tenure of office depended on the unpredictable outcome of the local elections, were anxious to have their proposals finalised and submitted to the Minister of Education as soon as possible, and they put together successively four possible schemes of reorganisation, none of which met with the approval of the teachers' representatives. At this stage, no doubt exasperated by what they considered to be the teachers' intransigence, they invited the teachers' representatives to prepare a scheme of their own, and granted us leave of absence for three weeks to do so. During that time we met at the Education Office, inaccessible to our colleagues left behind in school, and prepared a scheme which was mainly a two-tier system, avoiding large or difficult groupings. The Education Committee then decided upon their own scheme, which was approved by the City Council on 19 October, 1964.

It was now open to us to register our objections to the Minister of Education before it was approved by him in whole or in part. This we did, and were invited to submit them in writing, and to support them later in conference with the Minister or his representative.

We divided our case into four submissions, one for each Association to present their individual concerns, and travelled to London in the late spring of 1965. The meeting took place in a building in Richmond Terrace, off Whitehall, the stately proportions of which were compatible with its use by government. Our conference room, large, lofty, and furnished in the grand manner, would be a deterrent to the long-winded. Our Chairman and host was Reg Prentice, second in command to the Minister Anthony Crosland, and later to cross the floor of the House of Commons to join his erstwhile opponents on the Conservative benches. He was supported by a Ministry team. As we made our submissions, our eloquence was interrupted more than once. The Parliamentary Labour Party of the time survived on so slender a majority that a division in the House of Commons required the attendance of every Member. As one of us reached a vital passage of our statement, the door would open and a secretary would call out, 'Mr Prentice, the bells have rung'. He would leave the Chair with agility, returning some twenty minutes later. During one of these enforced intervals, a bespectacled civil servant, who out of doors must have worn a bowler hat and carried a rolled-up umbrella, remarked, 'This indeed reveals the disadvantages of split premises.' As we returned on the night sleeper to Liverpool, we had little expectation that our arguments would affect the substance of the Authority's proposals.

As indeed was the case. Though the Secretary of State's approval was generally subject to the completion of building improvements, by the end of 1968 fifteen comprehensive schools had been opened, with the long-term aim of providing twenty-eight schools for pupils aged eleven to eighteen.

The apprehensions of the Labour Party about their security of tenure were justified when in 1967 the Conservative Party won control of the City Council, and embarked on a damage limitation exercise in secondary education. The completion of the formation of the Quarry Bank and Holt

Comprehensive Schools was called into question, but the advice that the schemes were too far advanced to justify the ensuing disruption was accepted. Nevertheless the existing reorganisation proposals were withdrawn, and meetings of the Working Party, with changed political representatives, spent much time in considering the merits and demerits of various types of secondary reorganisation. The future of secondary education in Liverpool had become, for the time being, a political football.

The comprehensive story would be incomplete without reference to the voluntary (Church) schools. Roughly one third of secondary school children in Liverpool attended Roman Catholic schools. Although the expenses of the voluntary schools were largely met from public funds, they had the legal independence within the state system to make up their own minds about reorganisation. The Roman Catholic Archdiocese, free from the pressures of local politics, were able to spend as much time as they wished over their deliberations and planning. A Working Party was set up which, taking account of the complexities and upheaval involved in imposing a viable comprehensive organisation on existing school buildings, issued detailed Reports in 1974, 1976 and 1977. These provided the information base on which their secondary schools were reorganised step by step over a longer period.

The remaining three or four other voluntary schools stayed outside the new set-up, and attracted pupils from homes which disliked the comprehensive system. In the course of time parental choice enabled these schools to take the place in the city's education service which had been occupied by the old established grammar schools, the Collegiate and the Institute, which now lost their identity as part of the comprehensive system. In 1991 St Margaret's C of E High School had a Sixth Form of one hundred and fifty six, and the Blue Coat School a Sixth Form of two hundred and eight, according to a schools survey.

As this controversy in the maintained sector took its course, generally at the round table in the Small Committee Room, life went on outside. A major event was the retirement of the Director of Education, Harold Magnay, in January 1964. Appointed immediately after the war, his commission was to put into operation the Butler Education Act of 1944, then fresh from the printing press. At the end of his eighteen years' tenure he could claim to have implemented every requirement of the Act in whole or in part. His active interests had extended beyond the Liverpool education service to the support of voluntary youth organisations, and to the expression of his Christian faith by taking part in public occasions - the Annual Service for school leavers in the Cathedral, and broadcasts on television as a Free Church Christian. His presence at a succession of school and professional occasions outside working hours was beyond the requirements of his office. Teachers remembered him for his entertaining after-dinner speeches, when he was an expert performer. He often sent spontaneous laughter rolling round the tables. After his death in 1971 a memorial service in the Lady Chapel of the Anglican Cathedral paid tribute to the magnitude and diversity of his achievement.

He was succeeded by C.P.R Clarke, M.A.,B.Litt. Charlie Clarke, as he was known to his senior colleagues, was a Liverpool boy, who had joined the Liverpool education service in 1945 and, after a period in the Further Education department, had been appointed Deputy Director in 1952. He was to be Director for eleven years. To follow Harold Magnay would have been a demanding challenge, and it was perhaps appropriate that, except for his complete commitment to the exacting demands of his office, his personality was a contrast to that of his predecessor.

At Gilmour, as the years went by, I was glad to be a member of a lively community. The school's reputation had attracted a competent staff. The new Fifth Form of some fifteen boys did well in external examinations. Invitations as chief guest were accepted on two occasions by the Lord Mayor of the year. Projects would sometimes attract public attention. The Time Capsule, devised and assembled by the History Master, was a large bottle containing a map of the district, boys' essays on contemporary life in Allerton and Garston, a copy of the Liverpool Echo, and samples of small objects in daily use. It was sealed in the science laboratory and buried on the school site in the presence of the local press and with the help of workmen employed nearby. We liked to think it would engage the attention of an archaeologist in the distant future. It was a matter of differing conjecture between us as to what conclusions he, or she, would draw.

During the closing years at Gilmour we were involuntary players in a drama written by others. There was a sense of frustration for those, who by long service, had come to care for the school. In January 1963 the Education Committee had approved extensions which were to treble the size of the building. The work, which was to take two and a half years, began in November 1964. We were to have an Assembly Hall, a Dining Hall with kitchen, a Gymnasium, three Science Laboratories, two Woodwork Rooms, two Metalwork Rooms, a Geography Room, an Art Room, and a Lecture Room. There was general jubilation. We would no longer be a Cinderella building and would be able to offer to parents the best modern facilities for their children. Our fate in the coming comprehensive reorganisation was still unclear. But as the Education Committee's proposals became known, it was discovered that we were to be one wing of a group of three, with the neighbouring Gilmour Girls School and the New Heys High School for girls, a quarter of a mile away across the main road, Mather Avenue. The new school would be called New Heys and the name Gilmour would lapse. The planners suggested, by implication, that, although two of the three units carried the Gilmour name, its association with the secondary modern sector was one they were content to discard.

The Comprehensive School was to open in September 1967, and we arranged our programmes accordingly. The annual school magazine was issued at the end of the spring term, and the Head of English and the Head of Art decided to make the last number a worthy finale. As my contribution was insignificant, it is a pleasure to record that it was a model of its kind. A copy of Number 3 of the Gilmour Review, issued in June 1937, price twopence, which has survived, carried fourteen pages and was a worthy innovation at the time. Number 20, at Easter 1967, had one hundred and eight pages in three parts, the work and activities of the school, pieces written by the boys, and 'the old school'. Part three, which looked back in articles by former members of staff and former scholars, showed pride in past achievements, and was a fitting, and sometimes moving farewell to the Gilmour story.

The new building was officially opened on 4 May 1967. The ceremony, arranged by the Education Office, took place in the new Assembly Hall. Mrs. Ethel Wormald, now at the end of her two periods of tenure as Chairman of the Education Committee, led a strong platform party, including the chief guest and opener, Alderman W.H. Sefton, leader of the Labour City Council, the Director of Education, and representatives of the architects and builders. An impressive brochure gave an illustrated description of the new premises, and of the administrative processes required before building could begin.

At this ceremony I was in the unusual position of being also the Head of a school which existed only on paper. For the two or three comprehensive schools which had already been opened the Authority naturally sought Heads with comprehensive experience. There were none such in Liverpool, and secondary Heads, unless they were prepared to move elsewhere, had to accept that in the new schools they would revert to a less exalted status, under Heads recruited from outside. The outlook, particularly for secondary modern Heads, was not promising, and I was fortunate to be appointed to a proposed comprehensive school to open in September at the beginning of the Autumn term.

The Finch Hall Secondary Modern Schools and the Dovecot Secondary Modern Schools were situated on the city's eastern boundary on either side of the East Prescot Road, the Dovecot Schools in two separate buildings, one for boys, one for girls, the Finch Hall Schools in one large building, mainly single storey, round three quadrangles. An unseen but unchallenged frontier divided the building into two, each half a mirror image of the other, one for the boys, one for the girls. Built in the post-war era of slum clearance to provide for children of displaced families, the building had been englarged and modernised three years previously to offer a wide range of rooms and equipment for secondary education. There was now accommodation to spare, and reorganisation suggested the transfer of the pupils from the Dovecot Schools to Finch Hall.

The Finch Hall School was on the edge of its admission area. The Liverpool/Lancashire boundary ran across the playground, an anomaly which was to bring trouble in the future. Housing was entirely council provided. In the view of teachers and social workers it was a difficult area. Households varied from the law-abiding and thrifty to the lawless and spendthrift. There was constant feuding among some neighbours. If the school caretaker replaced old rubbish bins with new ones, the new ones disappeared overnight. It must be granted that old ones were left in exchange.

It was a common device of administration, when a school or other institution, deservedly or not, had 'got a bad name', to change it, when the opportunity arose, for a new one, regardless of the fact that the new name in due course found the level of the old one. So the Finch Hall Schools became the Yew Tree Comprehensive School, over whose birth I was now to preside.

THE COMPREHENSIVE SCHOOL

Appropriately the birth was accomplished by a man and a woman, a part-time secretary and myself. From 1 May, with a view to opening at the beginning of September, we were given a room in the Finch Hall Boys School, where, though I was a daily reminder of their coming demise, I was not made to feel unwelcome.

There were to be some seven hundred and fifty boys and girls from the four contributing schools. For their education there was available a building, of neglected appearance from the outside, but the modern interior was a testimony to the Authority's duty to provide first-class facilities irrespective of social background. At the current staffing ratio of 18.2 scholars per teacher, a staff of forty-one awaited appointment, from Deputy Head to probationer teacher., Building up a staff was to take all of the two and a half months of the summer term. Advertisements, applications, short lists, interviews. Interviews required the attendance of Governors and, for senior appointments, meetings at the Education Office.

What subjects would we teach, and with what priority? The accepted view at the time was that this was the Head's unchallenged domain. In practice, the right of the scholar to an all-round education, the career market, the requirements of civilised society, the availability and job satisfaction of staff, had their proper place in the final choice.

So to the time-table. Here I was a novice. At Wellington Road and Gilmour the Deputy Head drew up the time-table, and I had seen no reason to interfere. Now I was in at the deep end. On a day in September, some eight hundred people would arrive requiring a work programme and work rooms for a five day week. Staff help was not available - the summer term with examinations and leaving testimonials was the busiest of the three, and those who had been appointed were still fully occupied in their own schools.

From the beginning of schools and schooling, the time-table had been a decisive measure of success or failure in a school's business. It was the single most important operation of school management. From the age of eleven to sixteen the boy and girl have become a different animal, needing programmes different in scope and composition. A hundred and eighty scholars of a single age group present all grades of ability from the slow to the bright. Some subjects require longer or shorter lesson periods. Movement in the building at change of lessons should be as quick and easy as possible. The allocation of non-teaching time to staff should be fair, providing for their responsibilities outside the classroom. And so on.

Perhaps as a side effect of the current aversion to 11 plus selection, there were some in the profession who made known their objection to streaming within a school. Under this arrangement a hundred and eighty scholars on admission would be tested and put into classes according to their ability - 1a, 1b, 1c, 1d, 1e, 1f. They would take all lessons in these class units, with the same grading and description in succeeding years. This made for easier teaching. A narrow ability range in a class required a narrow range of lesson content at the appropriate level. But, said the advocates of mixed ability classes, this does the damage of 11 plus selection within a school. The F stream is permanently labelled as unable to cope and stops trying, and comes to accept that it must always be bottom of the heap. Each class, in their opinion, should present a cross-section of the entire ability range. Invidious and damaging distinctions would thus be avoided.

My own bias was in sympathy with the mixed ability advocates. Experience, then of more than thirty years, had led to the belief that schools could, and often did, give many pupils the idea that in the ability stakes they were the also-rans, undermining the self-confidence necessary for success. This, of course, was not the intention, but the difficulty of the majority with English spelling, with mathematical processes, and with the academic content of other subjects, accompanied by the daily criticisms, kindly or not, of the teachers, had, I considered, this harmful lasting effect.

But I knew also that to teach mathematics, science, a language, and some English, to a mixed ability class was not a practicable proposition. A process would be grasped right away by the few bright, after a period of trial and error by the average, and never by the few backward. How could a lesson under these conditions be conducted successfully by one teacher? This, however, did not apply to other subjects. Academic ability was not a requisite in, for example, the Crafts, (Woodwork, Metalwork, Cookery, Needlework), Art, Physical Education, Games and Music. Why not then have streamed (selected) ability groups for the academic subjects and mixed ability groups for the rest?

This was done. The school was organised in such a way as to draw the minimum of attention to the differing abilities of the pupils. The classes, now called Forms, were described by the initial letters of the school address. There could be no prestige in belonging to 1y rather than 1t. On admission the intake of one hundred and eighty was tested. This supplied the information to ensure that from the first year each Form carried a complete cross-section of the ability range. These Forms were the school unit to which the pupil belonged. Each Form had a Form Master or Form Mistress to whom the scholar could refer. At the beginning of each morning and afternoon the scholars assembled as Forms in their Form Rooms for registration. They were their classes for the non-academic subjects, which occupied more than half of their time-tables.

The entrance tests also provided the information to enable the first year group to be streamed into sets according to their academic ability. At certain lesson times, and these were fewer in the weekly time-table, the pupils would assemble in the graded Sets for Mathematics, Science, Modern Languages, instead of in the Forms to which they belonged. After the summer examinations, and taking account of teachers' reports, a pupil could be moved to a higher or a lower Set for the following year

On these lines the time-table was gradually built. I found it was like packing a suitcase for a holiday. The first items went in with care-free gusto. Early snags were easily dealt with, but they increased in difficulty, until finally one had figuratively to sit on the lid. The weekly time-table cards for forms, sets, and teachers were finished at home during the summer holiday. In my darker moments I imagined first day collisions with two classes attempting to occupy the same classroom. With my elder daughter, then aged thirteen, a demanding process of check and counter-check was devised.

During the Yew Tree years, as experience gathered, we found that time-tabling had to begin in the autumn for the following September, a year long process beginning with the assembling of Staff requests, and ending with the final time-table cards. In order to keep my feet on the ground I had always taken some part in class teaching. I chose a Third Year group of slow learners for English. When, after four years, I handed over the time-tabling to the two

Deputy Heads, I offered to continue this small contribution. After a couple of years they dropped me. Were they being considerate? Or did they think I was past it? Happily the age of computer time-tabling, if it really works, did not overtake me. Is it possible to program against Mr. A working alongside Mr. B, with uncertain consequences?

The requirement of distinctive school clothing for boys and girls demanded attention. School uniform, as it was described, was not a problem in grammar and independent schools, regarded there as a status symbol. In secondary modern schools it was less easy to establish. Parental indifference in some homes made it difficult to enforce against the natural wish of adolescents to break away from tradition. As time passed, I had come to the conclusion that effective education required the school to be interested in what the scholars wore, and to insist on standards. Distinctive school clothing, smart in appearance, established a bond between the scholars, and helped to foster a corporate spirit. But its negative advantages were more important. If left to their own choice, secondary school children, in their instinctive drive to become adults, were at the mercy of fashion, and would choose garments of exaggerated colour and design. They would compete with each other, extending with girls to the wearing of make-up and jewellery. It was noticed that, in these matters, most pupils would try to deceive their parents, saying that 'everyone else in the class is wearing it'.

The teachers' view was that children spent most of their time out of school, when their clothing preferences could have all the scope that the family budget could afford. The time for clothing adventure was in the evening, at the week-end, and during holidays. Indeed at school dances it was a pleasure to see the boys and girls so well turned out. But in the school working day it was a distraction and a source of rivalry and jealousy. The establishment and enforcement of standards was a long term operation. Without constant supervision a short period would see the adoption of teen-age fashion wear - high heels, leather coats, earrings exaggerated hair-styles. So they were told that they should dress suitably for their work and that school uniform was the best way to achieve this. The uniform was to be kept in good condition and changed when they got home. They should realise that it was an item in the home budget. Though the majority of homes welcomed this in principle, many seemed unable to influence their children's choice of clothing after the age of thirteen.

I recall a boy of fifteen appearing in school with a green stripe in his hair. He came to see me. The conversation on both sides was restrained and courteous. Why, he asked, should he not have the hair style he wanted? I said that this would lead to others adopting similar styles. Overall, round the school there would be a rainbow effect. "Why not?" he went on. He seemed to look forward to such an arrangement as a commendable embellishment of the school scene. But, I countered, parents generally were not as broad-minded as he and I. They would not want to send their children to a school where the standards they wanted were not maintained. As with such encounters between gentlemen, a compromise was agreed. He would not continue colouring. But the stripe would be left to die away from natural causes. A similar compromise was accepted in the school. It became the rule that uniform was worn during the first two years. Thereafter liberty was accompanied by due restraint.

The arrival of the first day had some resemblance to a birth - expected over a period with concern, and with relief and pleasure when it happened. Most of the Staff had not met each other before a Staff Meeting the previous day. It took a week or more for them to become acquainted and to find their way about the building. It did not take that long for the pupils of the Third and Fourth Years to realise that supervision in a large building was less effective than in the smaller buildings to which they were accustomed. They felt, too, that they were birds of passage, and could not identify with a school they were soon to leave. The first two years were a time of stress, the restlessness of the seniors involving the management in a heavy workload.

The pace of change was reinforced by the appointment of new Governors. Labour's three year term of office was broken in 1967, when the municipal elections brought in the Conservatives for a four year period. This meant a new Chairman and a membership which could provide the right majority. The new governors exercised their authority with a commitment which reflected their years in the wilderness. The Annual Open Day and Prizegiving had previously been the sole concern of the school. It was the Head's privilege to compose the guest list. I was told that the Governors wished one of their colleagues to be given platform time. Speech Days, in an era of entertainment by television, were for parents a duty rather than a pleasure - the Chairman's introduction, the Head's report, the address by the chief guest. The additional speech tested endurance to the point where some members of the audience were leaving before the end. It was clear that if this procedure were continued, attendance would decline at this most important occasion of the school year, when the work of all Departments was on display. On future occasions the platform was dispensed with, and after visiting the subject rooms the parents came to the senior Assembly Hall for drama, dance, and music.

The establishment of a channel of communication with the parents was now familiar ground Suggestions from the Heads of the contributing schools brought together parents from some half-dozen homes. I met with these regularly at school in the evening, providing the necesssary link between the school and interested parents. As far as they could, within the limited support they received, they arranged events to attract the interest of other parents, and to assist the school with finance and equipment. After some five years, co-operation between parents and school was strengthened by the active involvement of members of the teaching staff, resulting in the Parents' Committee being absorbed into a Yew Tree School Association of parents and staff.

The approaching half-yearly examinations called for the drafting of a scholar's report. I was concerned that it should reflect effort as well as standard reached. The publication of an order of merit based on examination marks had recently seemed inappropriate and divisive. The top few, year by year, were at the top, sometimes by native ability rather than hard work. The bottom few, sometimes after a term's steady work, were at the bottom. In spite of the misgivings of the traditionalists, on the report page the subjects were accompanied by two columns, one for attainment, one for effort. Instead of marks five grades A to E were awarded. The scholars were told that an A for effort was regarded as highly as an A for attainment. The reports were housed, year by year, in one sturdy folder, and at the end of their school life provided the story of their response and achievement.

Immediately after the reports were given out in January and July, on an evening, and if necessary the following afternoon, parents were invited to school to discuss their son's or daughter's report with the appropriate teachers. This was a most satisfying occasion In the Senior Assembly Hall, where the teachers sat at their desks, there was a buzz of conversation. The last teachers left around 10 p.m., regarding their temporary popularity as a dubious asset. Parents and senior scholars, used to paid overtime as a national institution, found difficulty in believing that this was a voluntary service.

Towards the end of my tenure I was gratified by the number of parents who increasingly took advantage of this opportunity. We also had to recognise that interest lessened as leaving time approached.

Percentage of parents attending Reports Days January 1976

Year 1	82
2	76
3	74
4	72
5	65

During the first year we were surprised when the limited academic ability of our charges became apparent. Standardised entrance tests showed that 80% of the children on admission were below average in reading ability, and 90% in arithmetic. This unfortunate situation had to be accepted. A Remedial Department was set up, which did what it could to help a few of the most backward. But hammering away at the basic subjects with the majority, especially in their final years when protracted failure had brought frustration and rejection, would be counter-productive. It was decided for the lower half of the ability range in the Fourth and Fifth Years to provide a course which would prepare them, as far as possible, for their future role as home-makers, wage earners, and voting members of the community. It was called Home Career Citizen, and was initially the responsibility of the Senior Mistress. I was impressed by the scope and variety of the courses she and her assistants produced. Her suggestion that this work should become the responsibility of a Head of Department was taken up, and a Head of Social Studies was appointed to organise and administer it. He extended the courses by contacting many of the professional and voluntary workers in a wide range of social services in the city. Visits by the scholars outside school, and visitors to school with the appropriate experience, would deal with, for example, the Pop Scene (drugs, sex, crime), vandalism, the Media, Women's Lib., the problems of old age, mental health, physical handicap, racial discrimination. These courses made heavy demands on the staff concerned. They were rewarded by the interest and involvement of the pupils, who in turn appreciated their relevance to life after school.

Exciting, and, in our view, successful as the Social Studies courses were, we had no doubt that the backbone of the school's work was in subject teaching - the perennial challenge to the teacher of imparting knowledge, and teaching skills, by methods which retained the interest and co-operation of the pupil. The subjects - those with more timetable space were organised in Departments - were in the charge of a Head of Department or Head of Subject. This was a welcome challenge to the experienced teacher. They had to have the academic respect of their colleagues in the Department, a command of method, the experience to use internal and external examinations in the interest of the scholar, an alertness to modern developments in the subject, and the ability to coach their staff into an effective teaching team. After seven years they were able to offer a small number of candidates for Advanced Level and Ordinary Level G.C.E., and 70% of the Fifth Year for the Certificate of Secondary Education, in which 70% of the 123 candidates passed at the various grades.

The school was just over a year old when the problems of the first two years were aggravated by the withdrawal of teachers from mid-day meals supervision. The 1944 Education Act had made school dinners an integral part of the school day, and Ministry Regulations had committed teachers to their supervision. Dinners were taken in two sittings, each hosting about one hundred scholars supervised by one teacher on rota, and three local ladies who had children in the school. In 1968 supervision by teachers became voluntary, and the Yew Tree Staff withdrew from it forthwith.

I had every sympathy with them having long been critical of this unpaid overtime. But the prospect of children, after a morning of classroom constraint, being released a hundred at a time to the care of three mums was alarming. The normally well-behaved would be noisy, sometimes quarrelsome. The disruptive would have a field day. I reported the situation to the Governors and to the Local Authority. The lack of response led me to undertake the personal supervision of both sittings during the Autumn Term, and of the first sitting only during the Spring Term. At the end of the Spring Term I withdrew, and reported to the Governors: 'I have withdrawn from direct personal supervision of the mid-day meal, which is now exercised by three lady helpers. I commend the efforts of these ladies to discharge their duties, but they have a task beyond their capabilities and cannot maintain control. The conduct of the meal is disorderly, ill-mannered, and dirty. On the recommendation of my professional association I have to point out that I cannot be responsible for the control and safety requirements of the children concerned.' Again there was no response.

The Authorities, however, were not always as oblivious to teachers' immediate needs as some of us in moments of despondency imagined. In the Autumn Term of 1973 we first heard of positive discrimination. This nugget of administrative vernacular described an initiative to provide schools in areas of social deprivation with extra finance. We decided to use it to strengthen our pastoral care. This expression, which made its appearance at the same time as the large comprehensive schools, meant treating pupils as people and not only as lesson fodder. It had been exercised informally in the smaller schools of the past as a natural reponsibility of the teacher. In the larger schools, where a child lost some of the notice which was a welcome by-product of the smaller community, additional attention was required to this aspect of child care. More so in a neighbourhood where families laboured under the stress of low incomes, and where standards were often poor.

Pastoral care had already been made a duty of Form Teachers and Year Teachers. Year Teachers - one for each of five Years - were experienced teachers who were given non-teaching time to enable them to organise meetings and events which would respond to the outlook of the age group, and to deal with scholars' problems referred to them by the Form Teacher. Some schools aimed to make the same provision by a House system. The school would be divided into a number of Houses containing all age groups, which would compete in games, athletics and other contests. The Year system, in our view, had two advantages. The approach to scholars could be pitched to the psychology of the age group, and Year Meetings could be held without disturbing the rest of the school.

So our extra money was spent on the appointment of a Head of Lower School (First and Second Years). a Head of Upper School (Third, Fourth, and Fifth Years), and a Co-ordinator of Sixth Form Studies. These senior teachers, in the sphere of pastoral care only, operated as Heads of their staff of Year Teachers. The main work of the Sixth Form Co-ordinator was to advise his small Sixth Form on the approach to a preferred career, or Further or Higher Education. The school had now two independent and complementary structures - subject teaching and pastoral care. The latter reinforced the former. Staff, to a greater or lesser degree, would be involved in both. It was an organisation which put into practice the precept that education is more than instruction.

While the organisation of pastoral care provided for the referral of troublesome children to Year Teacher and Head of School, its lengthy procedure was not an effective deterrent of disruptive pupils in the classroom. Since the beginning of schools the cane had successfully fulfilled this function. The Roman poet Horace described his schoolmaster Orbilius as 'plagosus' - prone to beating. Nearly two thousand years later in England there was a change in public sentiment. Though most parents, in our experience, wanted their children to be disciplined, in the professional and daily press articles appeared critical of corporal punishment, reinforced by a campaign organised by a small group of teachers. No-one, as far as we were aware, was prepared to defend it in public, with the risk of being labelled a flogger. The correct postures seemed to be the monopoly of one side of the argument.

Secondary children, when they became aware of this movement, were naturally not slow to take advantage of it. Caning, which had been accepted without demur, was now open to question. The Staff, too, felt their position to be uncertain, and though I assured them of my support, became hesitant to use the cane. I felt that disruptive children, some of them encouraged by their families, and having no regard for the advantages of a favourable school report, should, in the interest of class and teachers, be removed from the classroom. Where to? Could a suitable room be set aside for this purpose, where the basic subjects only would be taught, and return to the classroom and the various school activities be made subject to an undertaking of good behaviour? Would there be a teacher available for this work, which could be successful only if administered by one person? An experienced Master on the Staff was ready to oblige. The duty was combined with the maintenance and oversight of pupils' records, now numbering some nine hundred and fifty.

The Adjustment Class performed its function well. After the pupil concerned had been interviewed by the Year Teacher and the Head of School, the final decision, which I retained, was a formality. Before joining the Adjustment Class the child came to see me. I went over his/her record and pointed out the damage they had done to the progress of their schoolmates and to themselves. It was an occasion which, hopefully, made a necessary impression. The diversity of these cases was illustrated in a year's sample of twenty three boys and five girls. The five girls were supervised by the Senior Mistress. Three boys were transferred to other schools, two were put into community care, four reached the school leaving age, ten were partially, and four were completely, returned to the normal timetable.

While welfare, and the supervision of difficult pupils were the concern of the pastoral staff and the management, subject teaching in the Departments year by year became more firmly established. External examination results by pupils below average on entry testified to the efforts of the teachers concerned. Of the few Advanced Level subjects taken, some were in the higher grades. The Art department attracted attention for the quality of its work. The Head of Art must have felt that his approach was right for his pupils when two Sixth Formers were accepted by the Liverpool College of Art and Design, which, drawing from the whole of the North West, had a high standard of admission. On Open Days he had a bonanza. His subject was a natural for display and the Art Room was crowded. How could the Mathematics Department compete? It was helpful that the finance provided by the national Exchequer and the Local Authority for books, apparatus, and materials was more than adequate Each summer term for the following year I was able to meet the requests of all Departments in full.

I wondered, from time to time, how much the school's performance was affected by the frequency and damage of forcible entries into the building in the evening, at week-ends, and during holidays. In 1968, at the end of the first year, I reported to the Governors, the Director of Education, and the Chief Constable:

Easter Holiday

Gardener's shed entered and contents damaged.
Intercom wiring cut.
Gym Mistress's room entered and articles stolen.
Cookery store window broken and crockery smashed.
Biology Lab. window broken and apparatus damaged.
Staff room and kitchen entered and crockery broken.
Seven classroom windows and one glass door panel broken.
Maths store entered and equipment scattered on field.
Roof tiles pulled off and dropped on pathway.
Padlock on entrance gate broken.
Metalwork room entered and tools taken.

Half-term holiday

Forty nine windows broken.
Girls' gym store entered and equipment taken.
Twenty roof tiles pulled off and used to break wired roof glass over corridor.
Large plate glass window of Housecraft Room broken.

In my last Governors Report in 1976 the theme continued: 'During the Easter holiday seventy one panes of glass were broken from outside the building'.

During nine years the cost of repairs and replacements must have been many thousands of pounds. The building was surrounded by council houses, shops, and little else. When unoccupied it was an invitation to thieves and vandals. Juveniles were shielded from punishment by the Children and Young Persons Act. On a Sunday morning two boys, aged nine and seven, broke in, made their way to one of the Housecraft rooms, piled blankets on top of a gas cooker, and lit the jets. The room was burnt out. The boys were put under the care of the Social Services Department. The view in school was that the prospect of two or three strokes of the cane on the seat would have been an effective deterrent to them and others in the future. Sometimes adults were the culprits. The sports trophies were all taken on the same occasion from a display cupboard. A pane of glass was removed from the window of my room, the carpet rolled up and passed out to an accomplice. This would be done in the view of a row of houses, whose occupants did not wish to be involved.

The Authority went some way to institute safeguards. Some rooms were burglar alarmed, and some windows strengthened. Other measures were cosmetic. An elderly building patrol, police surveillance, which amounted to driving past the building. They would not hold keys,and if entrance was required had to go to the caretaker's house some distance away. On the Staff we could not understand the Authority's failure to take effective measures. Financially it would have paid to have employed two fit men at current wage rates to occupy the building when the school was not in session, with a set of keys and access to a telephone. Meanwhile teachers and caretakers were angry and frustrated to return to the school on Monday mornings and find windows broken, furniture damaged and equipment stolen, which took time to replace.

An added discouragement to pride in the school was the uncared for appearance of the playground, with grass and weeds between the flagstones. Regular reports to the Governors and the Authority were ineffective. It was necessary to apologise to visitors for this state of neglect. I wondered how many prospective parents and intending candidates for appointments had been put off after an exploratory visit.

The failure of the Governors to achieve improvement in these matters added to a growing disillusion with the value of the institution as it operated. In the independent sector the Governors had a role in representing the interests and traditions of fee-paying parents, and were in control of their own finance. In state schools they had no resources. Before the 1944 Act schools had functioned happily without them. The Act introduced requirements for school governance. All state schools were to have governors (secondary) and managers (primary). They were to be appointed by the Local Education Authority. The church schools appointed their own governors or managers, but representatives of the LEA had to be included. I formed the opinion that the opportunity of patronage thus made available to the political parties was what sustained the institution.

After working with three governing bodies, the nature, indeed in some cases, the existence of their qualifications was in doubt. Of equal concern was the absence of information as to how governors were selected, and by whom, information to which interested staff and parents were entitled. The majority were political appointments, and it seemed that the required qualification was service to the party. This, in my view, raised questions as to suitability.

Flaws in the selection procedure were matched by failings in the working of the system. Governors were empowered to make staff appointments and decide the priorities for minor building improvements. To carry out these responsibilities there were three termly meetings in the year, with special meetings, generally for appointments, as required. Governors were invited to the annual Open Day. This was the extent of their contact. No Governor, in my experience, asked to visit, to be shown round, and become acquainted with the school. Would Governors, in their own businesses or professions, have welcomed a lay body, visiting a few times a year, exercising control of their staffing and building priorities? Staff had legitimate grounds for complaint, in so far as Governors were not accountable for the consequences of their decisions. If an appointment turned out to be a mistake it was the school which had to cope. And the composition of the governing body was subject to change, as Governors withdrew and others took their place.

While the system was, in my view, ready for overhaul, any changes recommended should have made provision for legitimate parental concern and public interest. The selection procedure should have been made widely known in print to parents, teachers and the community. It should have been accepted that a lay body, with uncertain qualifications, was not fitted to make working decisions which affected the successful development of a school. Decision making, with its accompanying responsibility, and subsequent accountability, should have remained where it naturally belonged, with the school management. With this understanding, a consultative body of parents and citizens concerned with public issues could be formed. Meetings would include representatives of the school management, the staff, and the Education Authority. The role of such a body would be advisory only, but school managements would be expected to take due note of its views and recommendations.

Despite the handicaps, after the first two years the school seemed to mature. A Head, of course, sees his school through rose-coloured glasses. In moments of relaxation, perhaps taking tea with senior colleagues after school, he is prone to share his private thoughts - 'This is a good school. My administration is firm yet flexible.' (The Deputy Head on such an occasion, in the absence of the

Head, would enter a caveat - 'This could be a good school'.) But it was agreed that there was progress. The quality and stability of the staff was a decisive factor. The two Deputies and myself were together for nine years until my retirement, and some Heads of Departments did a similar stint. Sometimes we felt - was it imagination - that in an anonymous area of social deprivation we were an oasis of aspiration and endeavour. On occasion, inexplicably, there would be a shaft of light. It had been noticed that school parties on outside visits behaved themselves without strict supervision. On one occasion a lady came to the teacher in charge with £1.00 for the school fund 'because they were so good'. As the Annual Open Day and Prizegiving grew into a tradition, it became a measure of success. The work of the Departments was there to be seen and judged. At 8 p.m. parents and visitors, having toured the displays, gathered in the senior Assembly Hall, where the programme was planned as an entertainment. The distribution of prizes, which was limited to the Fifth and Sixth Forms, would be followed by a Dance Display by the girls.

In the finale I had a vested interest. Conscious of deprivation as a displaced teacher, I persuaded the contributing primary schools to make up a choir together with our girls and Lower School boys. We began combined rehearsals in January. My pianist was Warren Miles. Warren was unique in the profession for never having applied for a job. Without promotion ambitions he would stay at a school until it closed or was reorganised, teaching his preferred basic subjects to lower age groups, moving on as directed by the Education Office. He was a pianist and composer for the piano. Together we produced a programme, tuneful rather than sophisticated. To involve the parents the words of Bless this House were already on the chairs, and after the last choir item they were cajoled into joining in. I was glad to note that this did not affect attendance on later Open Days.

During my last year the school attracted some public attention, due, I confess, to my intransigence. When it was sited the planners had placed the building across the boundary between Liverpool and Lancashire, for reasons not now apparent. A school under normal circumstances, should be as near to the centre of its admission area as possible. Yew Tree's natural admission area was half in Liverpool, half in Lancashire. Previously this had worked to the satisfaction of both parties. Lancashire was short of school places, and paid Liverpool a per capita fee for their children attending Yew Tree.

By 1975 Lancashire's building programme had provided accommodation for all their resident school children. In July of that year I was instructed by the Liverpool Authority that Lancashire children from the primary schools were not to be admitted to Yew Tree the following September, and the parents were informed accordingly. This drew voluble and forceful protests from the parents concerned, who themselves, and their older children, and in some cases their parents, had attended the Finch Hall school since its opening in the 1930's. My sympathy with them was reinforced by time-table considerations. The time-table for the coming school year was now complete, after nine months' work by the two Deputies. The changes required by the reduction in numbers would have had to be made during the summer holidays, when the rest of the Staff were not available for consultation.

Spokespersons for the parents resident in Lancashire informed me that they would send their children to Yew Tree at the beginning of the Autumn Term despite instructions to the contrary. I did not discourage them. The children turned up, and week after week I personally made a separate record of their attendance, and they then went off to their classes. An Officer of the Lancashire Education Authority asked to come to school to address the parents, and this was done. To no effect. The press and television became interested, and while I refrained from entering the fray, they included their interviews with parents in the local papers and the current news programmes. After a term of these exchanges an agreement was reached. The children were to stay at Yew Tree and be put on roll. The following year the Yew Tree intake would not include the Lancashire children.

This protracted dispute, unwelcome as it was, went some way to divert my attention from the equally unwelcome thought that this year would be my last. Like many others I had regarded retirement as something which happened to other people

Decisions had now to be tailored to short term effects so as not to pre-empt my successor. Could it be that some senior staff at times seemed to be looking past me to a future in which I would not take part? Links would be snapped with daily companions, some of several years standing. Perhaps it was natural that those I would miss most would be my personal staff. My Secretary Irene Mason, who had been with me from the beginning. She had valeted me one afternoon before I left for my wedding ceremony. My cleaner, Mrs. Scott, who lived nearby, and like many cleaning ladies in Liverpool had a long association with her local school. The hours, early morning and late afternoon, did not interfere with daily housekeeping and shopping. Her strength of character, straight talk, and good humour, won general respect. Sometimes, by accident or design, when I arrived in the morning, she would be putting the finishing touches to my room. Her conversation, with a smile, was on the foibles of human nature. The brass door knob of the room reflected her attentions. I asked her if she would like it replaced with a plastic one. If that was done, she replied, she would only find something else to polish. One evening, after school, as I left my room, she was standing by a table in the entrance where a single hydrangea was illuminated by an overhead light. I joined her. After a silence she said 'Doesn't it speak to you.' I asked her what it said. Passing through a verse writing phase in retirement, I remembered the incident.

The Hydrangea

educated
with a fine tuned mind
he stood near Martha
swarthy and sweaty
leaning on her brush
by the school table
where the lit hydrangea
shone a thousand slanting shades
of blue blue symmetry

no words until
doesn't it speak to you

he answered
what does it say Martha
tell me and we both will know
what beauty is
and truth
maybe

The last day was not as trying as I had feared. During the preceding fortnight farewells had been said. The Staff had hired the banqueting room at Reynolds Park, Woolton, for a retirement dinner. They, the parents, and the scholars, had been generous with parting gifts. Before dispersing for the summer holiday there was the inevitable point of departure, the last assembly. After the Upper School and the Staff had taken their places in the Hall, a prefect came to say that all was ready. As he and I walked together through a silent school, I remembered that platitudes, and emotion unfamiliar and perhaps embarrassing to youngsters, must be avoided.

I had offered a farewell gift to the Staff, and was invited to attend their own staff meeting at the end of the day to present it. I made the presentation, but did not linger in the Staff Room afterwards. Returning to my room through a building occupied only by cleaners, I collected my things, and went out to the car, feeling strange.

LOOKING BACK

Since Plato, and maybe before, much has been written about education. The philosophers have looked at education as an idea to be examined, appraised, and assessed. For philosophers it has served as an abstraction providing a subject for their deliberations. They had in their minds a typical child of their time, without social disadvantages. In theory their doctrines could be applied by private tuition to a single receptive pupil. Valuable as some of their ideas have turned out to be, experience on the ground would have reminded them that education in schools is in classes, is a response to its society, and that it takes on the character of the society of which it is a part. Christianity, Islam, Communism, Fascism, have all educated their children in the light of their beliefs. Where there is no dominant creed, education takes on the colour of the institutions and culture of the society, and as the years pass, will sustain and reinforce them. If a society provides one kind of education for its ruling class, and another for the rest of its citizens, each part will take on its characteristic culture. The two will be strangers to each other, and the society divided.

A school can only operate in response to the purposes which its society, implicitly or explicitly, asks of it. Its task is easier when the society is agreed on those purposes. This is not always the case. To impart knowledge, to teach skills, to foster character, to inculcate beliefs, to turn out employees for commerce and industry, to establish habits of courteous behaviour, to kindle patriotism, to promote an international outlook? What should be the priorities?

One may glance in passing at the so-called progressive schools of the mid-century. A.S. Neill's famous Summerhill, where the pupils were a self-governing community. Bertrand and Dora Russell's Beacon Hill, where 'freedom given and understood early enough would result in a natural evolution to maturity and self-discipline.' Did their pupils, in later life, show discernible qualities of mind and character, distinct from those who had had a conventional education? Were such schools a well-meaning but misguided attempt to impose adult ideals on children in need of order, routine, and control?

What did parents require from a school? Generally, in secondary schools, the qualifications which lead to employment and hopefully a career. Few of us are good enough to place first the all-round development of the child. Indeed, the development of the child, for good or ill, is a balance between home and school. Reliability, tolerance, friendliness, and the growth of personality, are the province of the home. The work virtues, regular attendance, punctuality, application and co-operation in a team, are the province of the school.

Where did Yew Tree fit in to this pattern of schools and schooling? Did it fulfil the aspirations of the Liverpool Labour Party, which in the 1960's established the comprehensive schools? Their principal aim, to abolish the trauma of 11 plus selection, had been achieved. But the intention that the schools should carry a normal sample of the ability range, did not materialise. Either the majority of the children were below average in school subjects, or a number of parents were able to obtain admission for their children to other schools. This natural and legitimate exercise of parental choice eroded the performance of unpopular schools. A school might become unpopular as a result of unsubstantiated gossip. It was often concern for the well-being of their children in a suspect school, as much as the attractions of a preferred one, which decided choice.

The partial success of comprehensive reorganisation in Liverpool reflected the pattern of contemporary secondary education in the country as a whole. The comprehensive ideal was clearly affirmed by its advocates - that all children should be able to pass to well-staffed and well-equipped secondary schools, irrespective of ability or the financial status of parents. A government which had the means and the courage to establish, without loopholes, this basic human right would provide the building blocks of a loyal, undivided society.

There were two obstacles to this aspiration becoming reality - insufficient funding and the option of private education, better equipped and supported than the state system. Private education was exclusively for those who could afford it - the influential and knowledgeable, articulate in the expression of their concerns about their children's schooling. The inferior standing of the state schools was largely due to the absence of these parents.

There was no mystery about what made a good school. Buildings and equipment to modern standards. Staff properly qualified and committed to the service of their charges. This was the right of every school. But teachers might be in short supply, and, unhappily, some schools might attract good staff at the expense of others. What were the guide-lines for appointments? Not to be impressed by smooth talk, paper qualifications, and rapid movement from school to school. To look for steady service over a period, and a reluctance of the candidate's present school to lose him or her. The management? Teaching competence, experience, and academic achievement sufficient to command the respect of the Staff. In addition, the managerial skills - forward planning, firm but tactful administration, a disposition to keep staff informed of policy and developments, the ability to create a climate in which staff were content to work. A willingness to attract the co-operation of ancillary staff - caretakers, secretaries, cleaners, kitchen staff. A readiness to withstand the suggestions of the officers of the Education Authority - Advisers, Clerks of Works, Welfare Officers, and others - where the interests of the school required it.

It was a matter of opinion who was the more important for a school's success, the Head or the Senior Deputy. The Senior Deputy had to look both ways, to interpret the Head to the Staff and vice-versa, and, in addition to the special duties delegated to him or her, be prepared to deputise for the Head when absent. The Head - the Principal in school, the Ambassador outside. And here a hazard. This man with a commanding figure and resonant voice. That lady, tall, elegant, and beautifully dressed. Heads turn as they walk into a room, join the nearest group, and take over the conversation. They would impress visitors and parents on Open Day. Alas, these qualities were not reliable indicators of success. He turns out to be lazy, spends too much time out of school, and overworks his senior staff. They notice his late arrival to school in the afternoon after a lengthy lunch. She irritates with the latest gimmicks, and has favourites on the staff, with consequent prolonged friction and unrest. Appointment Committees, composed mainly of political nominees with a small minority of professionals, needed to give priority to more mundane and solid qualifications.

In later years one realised that to build a good school it was of no consequence whether it was in a favourable or an unfavourable area. Programmes and approach would be adapted to the character and potential of the neighbourhood. Good schools were developed over a period of years, the time it took to get together and hold good staff teams, to establish a tradition of co-operation between school and parents, and inevitably to imprint a character on the school which was the expression of the Head's philosophy of education.

The teachers? It was generally agreed that among the professions teaching was a poor relation. Not in the same class as medicine, or the law. For this there were many explanations. The shorter length of training - until 1960 non-graduate teachers qualified after two years at Training College. In an emergency, such as the shortage of men teachers after the war, one year's training was considered enough. The diversity of schools, from the village school to the grammar school teaching to Oxbridge scholarship standard, denied the possibility of a homogeneous profession. This led to different Unions representing sectional interests - the National Union of Teachers for its majority of women members, the National Association of Schoolmasters for men, the four grammar school Associations, the non-striking Professional Association of Teachers, the National Head Teachers Association. With differing interests they could not, and did not, speak to the employers and the public with one voice. The British Medical Association, on the other hand, represented a membership uniformly qualified by a mandatory period of training of five years or more. There were no one year emergency trained doctors. For these disadvantages the teachers could not be held responsible. Nor were they accountable for the preponderance of women in the profession, by nature adverse to public protest.

These considerations amounted to a handicap for Union leaders in negotiation. Public respect was there for Unions which could state their case and stand firm. To the bystander the profession seemed compliant - in putting up with political interference in matters of strictly professional competence, in accepting directions from Ministers educated at independent schools, who had little or no first-hand knowledge of the set-up and problems of the state school, in taking on unpaid duties, in receiving teachers, qualified by subject but untrained, into the classroom. Put into the equation the natural envy of teachers' holidays, and the unavoidable experience of some with an unpleasant teacher, and it was understandable that, sadly, esteem for the profession was in short supply. For the critics a short time teaching secondary classes would no doubt have redressed the balance.

Why then did we do it? Why did all but a few of us stay the course?

Job security, a guaranteed salary and pension structure, were no doubt the background, though not the starting point, for those who rejected the prospect of anxiety in these concerns. For the beginners after the first few years it was a welcome surprise that hours of work and long holidays offered a secure basis for family life. There was pleasure in passing on knowledge to willing listeners, sharpened by the quickness of the bright and the gratitude of the slow. There was a sense of achievement when examination results were good, or trophies won. Life in the classroom was relieved by many activities - games, clubs, visits, visitors, concerts, music and drama, camps, holidays abroad, open days. The occasional parent's letter of appreciation. And, as the years passed, the stimulus of daily contact with the young. I had drifted into a job which I liked, and which I came to respect. If the clocks turned back I would be content to travel the same road again.

TAILPIECE

Some years into retirement we were staying in Liverpool and planned a morning's shopping. Having become used to wearing a woolly hat to comfort the deficiencies of nature, I put it on, and to forestall objections said, 'No-one will recognise me now'.

In the stationer's shop in Slater Street, while I was being served, an assistant called out from the back,

'Excuse me, were you the Head Master of Yew Tree School?'

Feeling like a culprit caught in the act, I smiled and asked her her name. I apologised for not remembering her.

'You wouldn't, she said, 'I was one of the good ones. But you did send me to detention once.'

I registered regret.

'For giggling'.

I felt a monster. To change the subject I asked.

'Did we teach you anything?'

'Yes,' she said, 'I think so'.

ACKNOWLEDGEMENTS

To these authors for the use of their painstaking labours:

Keith Evans The Development and Structure of the English School System

H.C. Barnard A Short History of English Education

Robert R. Rusk The Doctrines of the Great Educators

To

Mr. and Mrs.S.W.Tiller and Mrs. Myra Fitzsimmons, for information otherwise unobtainable

The Roman Catholic Archdiocese of Liverpool

Mrs. Susan Johnson, daughter of the Rev.H.H.Symonds

Tony Williams, Librarian of the Liverpool Education Authority

Adrian Allan, Assistant Archivist, The University of Liverpool

Mary Gomez of the Liverpool Promotion and News Unit

My typists Kathleen Hodgson and Sally Meakin

My wife Margaret, for proof reading, and sustaining the role of writer's widow with fortitude and tolerance.

To

John Mills Photography Limited for photographs of school buildings.

APPENDICES

1. Chronology of schools

2. Percentage of admissions to selective schools from secondary modern schools 1954 - 1964

3. Comprehensive reorganisation - memorandum submitted to the Secretary of State by the teachers' representatives

4. The political control of the Liverpool City Council from 1956 to 1976

5. The teacher-pupil relationship

CHRONOLOGY OF SCHOOLS

1916 - 1919 Birchfield Road Council

1919 - 1921 Clint Road Council

1921 - 1929 Liverpool Institute Grammar

1932 - 1933 Liverpool University School of Education

1934 - 1935 Granby Street Council

1935 - 1938 Heyworth Street Council

1938 - 1939 Sefton Park Council

1945 - 1948 Earle Road Secondary Modern

1948 - 1954 Florence Melly Secondary Modern

1954 - 1958 Wellington Road Secondary Modern

1958 - 1967 Gilmour Secondary Modern

1967 - 1976 Yew Tree Comprehensive

THE ELEVEN PLUS

PERCENTAGE OF ADMISSIONS TO SELECTIVE SCHOOLS FROM SECONDARY MODERN SCHOOLS

Year	Number of selective places	Percentage of the age group
1954	2385	19.7
1955	2506	20.2
1956	2472	21.2
1957	2938	23.3
1958	3572	21.6
1959	3281	23.6
1960	3068	23.9
1961	3171	26.3
1962	3250	27.5
1963	3407	30.1
1964	3790	33.9

1964 In the maintained Secondary Modern Boys schools the percentage offered selective places was 40.6.

The 'eleven plus' was the examination taken by children at the age of eleven during their last year in the primary school, to select those who were suitable by ability to continue their education in grammar or technical schools.

THE CITY OF LIVERPOOL

THE COMPREHENSIVE REORGANISATION OF THE MAINTAINED SECONDARY SCHOOLS

Memorandum submitted to the Secretary of State for Education and Science

by

The Liverpool Teachers' Association
The Liverpol Association of Schoolmasters
The Liverpool Joint Four Secondary Associations
The Liverpool Head Teachers' Association
(statistics and details omitted)

Introduction

This memorandum summarises the views of the Liverpool teachers, expressed to the Officers of their Associations, on comprehensive reorganisation and the Authority's proposals.

The difficulties of reorganisation in Liverpool, and the objections already lodged to the Liverpool Plan, have been widely canvassed and are well known. We offer our observations to the Minister as the views of teachers of long experience in Liverpool, whose duty it will be to operate the reorganised schools.

Reorganisation and its problems

Reorganisation should aim at the maximum amount of social and educational justice. The bipartite system provided able children of all classes with educational opportunity, either through the 11 plus, through transfer to selective schools at 13 plus or later, and latterly through the development of successful G.C.E. streams in Secondary Modern schools. Reorganisation should achieve all this and more.

No one solution to the problems of reorganisation in Liverpool is immediately apparent:

Neighbourhoods perpetuate social and educational inequality in the background of certain areas.

Zoning to achieve cross sections of ability and social class appears artificial on the map, and unconvincing on the ground in some cases.

A uniform two-tier system appears to call for a linking of schools, which in some cases can be highly artificial if equality of intake throughout the city is to be achieved. Equality of intake is clearly linked with the maintenance and development of standards, and this in turn has effects upon the quality of staff which can be attracted and retained. In a comprehensive system it is important that there should be parity of opportunity between schools.

A uniform 11-16 system with one or two prestige sixth form colleges, meets considerable opposition from the teachers' associations.

The Liverpool Plan

The teachers appreciate the desire of the Authority to remedy any educational and social disadvantages of the bipartite system. They consider that the measures proposed, if carried out all together, at an early date, will do more harm that good to the children in the maintained secondary schools.

It would have been fortunate and extraordinary, if the school buildings of a County Borough of the size of Liverpool, built over a span of five or more decades to meet the requirements of earlier conceptions, were to be suitable for total change-over from a selective to a non-selective system. The proposals to do this by grouping together the existing buildings presents complex problems of organisation and daily operation. In the 'easier' groups the difficulties will be tolerable by skilful administration and the patience of staff. In the 'hard' groups the problems appear so involved and intractable as to make the unit unworkable as one school. Where a disproportionate amount of energy is to be absorbed in meeting these difficulties, schools will find it harder to support the normal trials of staff shortage and absence, the special problems of mixed school populations in the period of transition, and if teacher shortage develops further, a possible deterioration in staffing ratios.

The weaknesses of the proposed Liverpool plan are as follows:-

The application of a neighbourhood principle at present will cause inequality between certain zones.

It merges the identity of too many good schools, selective and non-selective, and disrupts the work of too many teachers. The scale of redeployment proposed would undermine the morale of the profession in Liverpool and would prejudice loyalties between colleagues and schools which have been built up over years.

It spells the ruin of two nationally famous Grammar Schools - the Collegiate and Institute Schools - and abolishes sixth forms of value, John Hamilton and Toxteth, which have developed a growing tradition of further education in the inner areas of the city. Ellergreen, which has pioneered an interesting variety of courses, and Aigburth Vale, a girls Grammar School with a high reputation in the city. Evered Avenue, a co-educational school which has proved very acceptable in its neighbourhood, is to disappear altogether.

It establishes two sixth form colleges, Hillfoot Hey and Childwall Valley, on very uncertain tenure in inappropriate areas.

It groups together the remaining schools, selective and unselective, in combinations which vary from the possible to the ridiculous.

The All-Through Comprehensive in separate buildings

The Authority favours this improvised and difficult form of organisation in the belief that it is the only system in the present circumstances which will provide continuity of curriculum, under the control of one Head, with subject Heads of Departments. The Teachers who have first-hand experience of working inside schools, have little confidence in the workability of a number of the proposed groupings.

Movement between buildings

The Authority suggests that the difficulties of separate buildings are not serious. The teachers consider this an optimistic view. Freedom of time-table depends on a surplus of accommodation over minimum requirements and a favourable staffing ratio. If time-tabling cannot deal with the problems of movement between buildings - and the teachers believe it cannot - there will be a loss of efficiency, in terms of time and energy, underestimated by the Authority.

Size and the school community

The teachers are concerned that, beyond a certain size - perhaps the accommodation of the main Assembly Hall - it becomes increasingly difficult to foster a corporate spirit and a sense of community; separate buildings aggravate this position so that loyalty to school is displaced by loyalty to buildings and to age groups, according to the number of buildings and their distance apart.

The Neighbourhood Principle

Under the present system, children from varied social backgrounds accept one another in school without question, on the playing field and in the classroom. A major disadvantage of the Authority's scheme where children from the more deprived areas are concerned is that the proportion of children who have gained selective places from different areas of the city varies according to the social background, and therefore able children in less affluent neighbourhoods may lack the stimulus in their new neighbourhood schools which they found formerly in the selective schools to which they were transferred by the 11 plus.

The loss of existing schools

Many of our members have been shocked that reorganisation will involve the running down and virtual elimination of established schools of merit, two of them nationally famous Grammar Schools, and there is widespread sympathy for our colleagues in these schools, many of whom have given their working lives to the task of enlarging and developing their schools to a high standard of performance, and who are rightly proud of the contribution of their former pupils - notably their Sixth Formers - to civic and national life.

The teachers urge that in any scheme of reorganisation, the strongest efforts shall be made to incorporate the academic potential of these schools into the new system, with the minimum of dispersal.

Coeducation

It must be noted that no evidence exists for any assumption that the general public share the enthusiasm of the Authority for this development. Generally, it is felt that the benefits of coeducation are strongest at Sixth Form level, and that during early adolescence there should be facilities for separate instruction, whether in single-sex schools, or by measures of organisation in a coeducational school. In future discussions a fuller consideration of this aspect of reorganisation would be welcomed by the teachers.

The Teachers' Policy

The policy of the Teachers' Associations is to aim at the establishment, by a process of orderly development, of a comprehensive system of secondary education in Liverpool, in furtherance of the present policy of the Department of Education and Science. To some of our members this represents the fulfilment of their own philosophy of education; to others it comes as a development which they would not have sought of their own volition, but we are united in the belief that a teacher's first duty is to the children in the schools, and that consideration demands our closest co-operation in making change effective with the minimum disruption to the progress and well being of the individual child. The immediate task would be to adapt the existing organisation to some modification of the present system which would command public respect, and which would not impose on good schools changes so fundamental as to impair the educational interests of existing pupils or the professional interests of their staffs.

The Associations representative of the Liverpool teachers have accepted the move towards the abolition of the 11 plus, and in considering schemes for secondary reorganisation, have also insisted on maintaining the best features of good schools of all kinds, especially the sixth forms in good schools of proven value at a time of increasing expansion in university and further education generally. This is clearly not the time to interfere too drastically with the sixth forms of well established schools. Emphasis should be placed on making the benefits of these available to more pupils.

Consultation

It is clear that the Authority and the teachers have had different views of the function and scope of consultation. In the Authority's view it is permissive - we were reminded that the Authority 'had no need' to consult us. The teachers regard it as obligatory for the Authority, and themselves, to approach a major enterprise such as this, in partnership and in mutual confidence. The teacher representatives consider that on the professional aspects of reorganisation full and proper consultation has taken place to date. On the educational issues it has been piecemeal and inadequate - the Authority preparing schemes separately, and calling one meeting on two-tier organisation before presenting two schemes for comment. In fact, the teachers' proposals were treated perfunctorily by the Authority, who appeared to be committed already to a time-table, and there was no opportunity for discussing the teachers' scheme in depth.

The Teachers' Plan

Copies of the Teachers' Plan prepared in September 1964 have been sent to the Minister. The teachers attach more importance to the views set out in the preamble than to the attached list of school groupings, which was produced under the pressure of a time limit in an attempt to minimise the disadvantages of the Authority's Plan. The weaknesses of the Teachers' Plan - two-year schools, low form entries - are manifest, but since the Authority at that time was committed to complete reorganisation by September 1965, our aim was to harness existing school organisation to the new system with the minimum of disruption, to provide schools of manageable size and a wider choice of single sex schools. These aims we advance as important considerations for future planners.

Proposals

(1) We request the Secretary of State to reject the present Liverpool Plan, and to urge on the Authority that it should resume discussions with the teachers with a new understanding of the scope and procedure of consultation.

(2) It should be accepted that reorganisation will be phased, and unsuitable projects deferred, pending the completion of adequate building plans.

(3) It should be accepted that the best solution to the Liverpool problem may be the development of a mixed system of reorganisation operating at different speeds and taking different forms in various parts of the city and the Authority should be asked to consider the desirability at this initial stage of variety and

experiment in forms of comprehensive organisation in preference to a uniform pattern of schools.

(4) We urge that the Secretary of State should not countenance destructive changes or too radical modification of any established school of proved worth.

(5) To provide a more informed background to local discussions, the Authority should be asked to prepare, with the teachers, one or two pilot schemes in considerable detail, preferably one for grouping of schools felt to be easy, and one where the suggested amalgamation would present difficulty. It would be advisable that Her Majesty's Inspectors should take part in these discussions.

(6) We request the Secretary of State that the sense of urgency and pressure be removed from all discussions; a good plan which has taken time to produce is to be preferred to one which is improvised to satisfy an arbitrary local timetable.

May 1965

THE POLITICAL CONTROL OF THE LIVERPOOL CITY COUNCIL FROM 1956 TO 1976

1955-1961	Labour		
1961-1963	Conservative		
1963-1966	Labour		
1967-1971	Conservative		
1972	Labour		
1973	Con. 9	Lab. 42	Lib. 48
1974	Con. 10	Lab. 42	Lib. 45
1975	Con. 14	Lab. 42	Lib. 43
1976	Con. 17	Lab. 42	Lib. 40

From 1973 to 1983 no party had an overall majority. In 1973, 1974, and 1975 the Liberal Party was the majority party and assumed leadership. In 1976 and 1977 the Labour Party assumed leadership, and chaired committees.

THE TEACHER-PUPIL RELATIONSHIP

Though gifts of personality are helpful, a successful and rewarding relationship can be built up by studying how children respond in the school situation.

The experience of one's own childhood is a guide to what children dislike in adults who supervise them — sarcasm, 'showing them up', ill temper, nagging, inconsistency in demands, favouritism. These faults occur more often when there is teacher fatigue and stress. Here organisation and preparation make a strong indirect contribution to good relationships.

What children like is not a good guide for effective teaching — they like to be amused and not worked too hard.

Consider what they respect and appreciate — professional competence, patience, fairness, understanding, consistency.

Children are people who happen to be young and inexperienced. They will appreciate it if instructions, of which they understand the purpose, are given in a clear and friendly way.

In matters of discipline firmness comes before friendliness.

September 1975

INDEX